# DIVING

## INTO THE

### Divine Feminine

**13 STEPS**

## TO FREEDOM FROM FOOD ADDICTION

# VYANA REYNOLDS

Cover Design and Interior Design by Kendra Cagle (5lakesdesign.com)

Published by 13 Step Press
Printed in the United States of America
ISBN:  978-0-9994597-3-7 (paperback)
ISBN:  978-0-9994597-7-5 (hardcover)
ISBN:  978-0-9994597-4-4 (eBook)


For permission requests, please contact
support@13StepPress.com

# Table of Contents

## STEP 1: *Surrender*

## STEP 2: *Compassion*

# STEP 3: *Know Thy Self*

# STEP 4: *Create a Life You Love*

# STEP 5: *Sovereignty*

# STEP 6: *Inspiration*

# STEP 7: *Fulfillment*

# STEP 8: *Rediscover Your Passion*

# STEP 9: *Reclaim Your Power*

# STEP 10: *Reconnect*
## WITH YOUR WISDOM

# STEP 11: *Connection*

# STEP 12: *Release*

# STEP 13: *Spiritual Transmutation*

# Acknowledgements

One of my favorite dreams began in the backyard of my childhood home, where I met two fairies in the form of small guinea pigs. They were clearly fairies, however, because I could see that one was wearing a string of pearls around her neck. Dead giveaway! They beckoned me to watch a TV show on the log in the backyard—they had a movie to share. The movie was black and white, appeared to be from the 1950s, and quite boring. It featured men and women in suits entering an important board meeting of some kind. The door to the meeting closed and the movie was over. I didn't understand why the fairies wanted me to see this movie until . . .

The fairy guinea pigs replayed the movie, this time with a color overlay representing what was happening "behind the scenes" in another dimension, but at the same time and place. Only the viewers of this movie could see the colorful fifth-dimension. It was hidden to the black and white world (representing our usual third dimensional existence). The colorful players looked like six humans who really were excited about the board meeting, had brought numerous exotic gifts for the participants, and wanted to share their enthusiasm, somewhat like cheerleaders. They, however, were not invited to the meeting at all, and when the door to the meeting closed, the only fifth-dimensional gift that made its way into the boardroom was a large orange bird that one of the colorful humans had brought. It flew in just before the doors closed.

I realized three important rules about the universe from this dream:

1. *The higher dimensions are not seen in the third, but are over-lapping and very interested in our well-being no matter how mundane it appears.*

2. *From behind the scenes, many beings are rooting for us, eager to lavish us with whatever we need to make our dreams come true.*

3. *Usually, they cannot "meddle" in our lives unless invited (no open door policy).*

When I awoke, I wanted desperately to know what happened at the board meeting. What was the role of the orange bird? The next night, before Dreamtime, I asked the fairies to take me back into the movie and show me what I desired to see. To my amazement, they did!

The orange fifth dimensional bird was perched (unseen) on the right shoulder of a man sitting at the head of the oval table in the black and white scene. At just the right moment, it whispered a creative idea in his ear. That creative idea was exactly what they needed at the meeting. He shared the idea with the group believing it to be his own.

I believe that's how most ideas and wisdom come to us—as gifts. They were never ours to begin with. The man who shared the idea in the boardroom can only take credit for being open to the gift and having the courage to share it.

It is from this place that I share this book. Nothing in this book is original. I believe that wisdom is timeless and belongs to the collective wisdom repeatedly remembered in different times, forms and cultures. You have access to all of it the same as me. I offer this book as a gift from the universe, not as a gift from myself.

After a lifetime of struggle and suffering, the wisdom in this book gave me freedom from food addiction in just 13 weeks. I offer it in hopes that it will transform your life as well. I included so much content that you can enjoy it buffet style—choosing the parts that really make a difference for you personally and leaving behind that which is not relevant to your life.

Having said that, I am so grateful for the blessings of the spirit that I continue to receive, and from what source they are gifted to me, including:

- **The Divine Feminine** that resides in the heart of all of us, who inspired me to arise every morning at 5 a.m. and write this book on the Big Island of Hawai'i.

- My wise parents, Ian Marsh & Connie Johnson.

- My husband, Bud Reynolds, for all his love and support.

- My fairy godmother, Ariel Spilsbury, and the 13 Moon Mystery School *(SanctuaryoftheOpenHeart.com)*.

- Jade Lotus of the Emerald Temple *(EmeraldTemple.com)*.

- Jumana of Aquamystica *(Aquamystica.com)*.

- My beloved mythic sisters/brothers who supported my path.

- Landmark Education and my many coaches *(LandmarkWorldwide.com)*.

- My estate planning clients of 20 years who at the doorstep of death brought me deep wisdom of life.

- Sacred writings of Christianity, Islam, Hinduism, Buddhism, Hawaiian spiritual traditions and the Baha'i Faith.

- PAX by Alison Armstrong *(UnderstandMen.com)*.

- As well as all the etheric beings behind the scenes that I have not met yet including guardian angels, fairies, mermaids, and unicorns.

# Introduction

Are you ready to go the distance to be free of food addiction? If so, then I recommend completing the 13 steps in 13 weeks by reading the daily affirmations, inspirational stories and applying the steps to your life. You will need to carve out at least one-half hour every day to complete the powerful practices in these steps. That may mean going to bed one-half hour earlier so you can get up earlier. Carving out a little quiet time in our busy schedules can sometimes be the hardest part of the entire program, and that's why I created the seven tips to getting up earlier (See Exhibit I).

## HOW THIS PROGRAM WAS BORN

Just before I wrote this book, I woke up with a sugar hangover after three bowls of sugar cereal and a bag of peanut butter M&Ms for dinner. I had a headache, a yeast infection and recurrent self-loathing for my apparent lack of discipline. I wondered in self-judgment, "Why am I sabotaging my life when I'm so blessed? I have no excuse for this kind of destructive behavior. When will I grow up?"

Food addiction runs in my family—and many of us have struggled with this for a lifetime. I've seen what it looks like at the end of this addiction—when someone I knew died in her bed, alone, over five-hundred pounds, unable to move from the weight. She didn't want visitors because she was ashamed of how far things had gone. She couldn't get up to use the restroom. She had bedsores and painful skin eruptions. The four paramedics that came to take her body away could hardly carry her body out of the door due to size. She was my age at the time (forty-five years old).

I had fat "rolls" around my middle for the first time, shortness of breath, I was the biggest I had ever been at one-hundred-seventy-six pounds—afraid to get on the scale again, and was feeling achy! The worst part was that I felt resigned about it.

Years ago, the traditional 12 Step program (originally created for alcohol addiction) provided hope from my resignation and some limited relief, but after 2 years of working the 12 steps my pattern of addiction continued.

The traditional 12 Step program, however, had 3 magic ingredients that REALLY worked for me—it provided a spiritual solution to a seemingly physical addiction, it provided community with authentic sharing and it provided an action plan to move out of the old pattern of addiction. However, after a couple of years of saying I was "powerless" over food and focusing on the problem during our meetings rather than focusing on the future we desired to create. I found myself unconsciously conspiring with others in the group, that I was a victim to addiction for life, and that the program could only help me cope. We kept focusing on the very thing we did NOT want to recreate!

I have come to believe that what we pay attention to persists and what we don't give our attention to falls away on its own. Therefore, I'm spending a lot more time visioning the future I want to create than remembering my past.

I tried hypnosis last year and one session lifted the veil of addiction for four months with no effort on my part, and then I relapsed once again. I thought there's something there—but how to make it sustainable. If my addiction is subconsciously driving my life, then addressing it with tools that influence the subconscious should assist tremendously. We will use affirmations daily in this program for this reason.

We will also use archetypal embodiment in these 13 Steps. Embodying archetypes is something humans do from time to time, when we're lucky, without even realizing it. It occurs when we step into a part of ourselves that is bigger than our individual personality. It's transpersonal. For example, when a man becomes King, he steps into a mythic life that is much greater than his personal needs and desires. He speaks for the entire kingdom and offers leadership. When Amma became the hugging saint, she stepped into her mythic life offering unconditional love and hugs to all of humanity. This path is much greater than her personality and is therefore incredibly powerful. Mythic figures are humans that embody archetypes such as the Shaman (indigenous medicine men & women), priest/priestess, jester/fool, Knights on mythic journeys, crones/Kahuna (wisdom keepers), kings/queens.

*I also recommend using color, essential oils, certain flowers/trees, intention setting, physical movement, healing modalities such as homeopathy and massage to assist our well-being.*

One morning, I woke up with a vision that offered another way out of my addiction—a path to freedom! I call it the 13 Step Program to Freedom.

The 13 Step Program emerges out of my training in a spiritual path that connects us to the Divine (Higher Power) from a feminine perspective.[1] These steps are inter-faith, so that anyone from any faith tradition could apply these steps and become even more deeply spiritual in their own tradition.

The 13 Step Program also takes its lead from the 12 Step Program created by two compassionate men who founded a spiritual path that followed 12 steps that they called Alcoholics Anonymous. The 12 step path is linear, focuses on "doing" the steps as mental practices and follows the analytical psyche. The 12 Steps works well in the American culture because it values DOING (action), linearity, and the masculine.

In contrast, the 13 Step Program is based directly on BEING—on mystical experience of the Divine, particularly the Divine's feminine qualities that so often get overlooked in our male-centered culture. I'm talking about love, compassion, surrender, intuition (inner knowing), stillness, dreaming, connecting, receptivity, release, softness, comfort in NOT knowing everything, acceptance, listening, creativity (art), synchronicity, and simply Being, to name a few. No one gets paid very much in our culture to just BE these qualities. Instead we reward mental intelligence, scientific method, power OVER nature or others, consumption, productivity and generally overdoing it (such as in extreme sports).

When we don't take time to cultivate our divinely feminine qualities, we don't give ourselves permission to balance out our Yang energy and **rest, reset, receive** and **recharge**. No wonder we all

---

[1] *I would like to express my gratitude to Ariel Spilsbury (www.holographicGoddess.com) and the 13 Moon Mystery School (http://sanctuaryoftheopenheart.com) for remembering our archetypal embodiment.  13% of all profits will be given to them.*

end up feeling exhausted and so many women have heart attacks. Overuse depletes our soil, overfishing depletes our oceans, our schools lack books and basic supplies, too many cars congest our streets, and we live on top of one another in little boxes on concrete slabs we call apartments—often feeling disconnected from the Divine and nature. No wonder we reach for food!

## THIS IS NOT A RELIGION

I strive to honor all religions in this process so that whatever religion you are when you arrive, you will feel encouraged to become even more deeply so. At the same time, my approach is more spiritual—a deepening rather than a "religion." I hope that we all can look at whatever beliefs are nurturing us, and whatever beliefs we may need to discard, if they are no longer serving us. We are all on an independent search for truth, rather than just believing what a guru or group of people may say is true. This is a path of freedo. Those, who prefer the rigidity that structure can often create, may not enjoy this particular ride. We are all on a ride through life; we may as well take the path that excites us the most. It takes a great deal of courage in a world that is perceived as dangerous to step out of the black and white, right and wrong, heaven and hell conversation. This path encourages self-reflection and a willingness to be in the paradoxical gray zone, the uncomfortable world of NOT knowing all the answers, in hopes of glimpsing truth with an open heart and mind. We may have to be reminded to say, "Trust the Process" every day.

I don't think of my work as religious, possibly others may perceive it differently. For example, we will be exploring what it would be like if we stepped into our own Divine magnificence from a feminine lens. Most qualities of the Divine feminine have been stamped out of religions for thousands of years and so most of us don't have a lot of experience with this. Right now, our currently male-focused world needs the power of the feminine for balance, but it can also feel like a threat to existing power structures. There is no need to perceive that there is a power struggle—just a reclamation of our feminine values, whatever they may be.

Feminine qualities inspire each of the 13 Steps. The first step, for example, embodies the qualities of motherhood—how we can be a Great Mother to ourselves. Knowing how humans love to put labels on things, I imagine some may call this work mystical, Jungian archetypes, sacred theater, new age, pagan mystery school, or Goddess worship because we are honoring the Divine feminine in each of us.

The 13 Steps are more accurately whatever you make them since YOU alone apply the steps to your life—no one else. With all things, including religion, I recommend taking what works for you and leaving the rest behind. Whatever choices you make are most valuable when made in alignment with your unique soul's journey.

## WHY 13 STEPS INSTEAD OF 12?

The number 12 represents the solar cycle—the masculine. There are 12 sun rotations in a year (if we add a few extra days to make that work). There were 12 apostles of Christ, all men. The number 13 represents the lunar cycle—the feminine. There are 13 full moon cycles in a year—exactly—and the female reproductive cycle follows it exactly—restarting every 28 days. The pope recently acknowledged

Mary Magdalene as the 13th apostle of Christ. How synchronistic that she, as number 13, represents the missing feminine in Christ's group.[2]

I spent most of my life valuing ONLY the masculine qualities and dismissing the feminine. Who needs rest anyway, right? No one is paid to sleep! That approach left me exhausted.

I'm so excited to apply this body of wisdom to my current state of affairs—my experience of life-long inherited food addiction. *I do not want my life to be all about food—how to get it, how to hide it and how to avoid it.* This program is one of wholistic spiritual trans-formation—it will transform your LIFE not just your relationship with your food and your body. We approach it as a remembrance of a way of BEING, not something you "DO" although ACTION in align-ment with your JOY is rewarded. When you feel joy, you can't help but do your happy dance. When that happens, you're moving in the right direction—enjoy the joy ride.

Powerful practices are suggested only to prime the joy pump and to clear things out of the way so joy can flow freely. *This pro-gram should be approached as play, not work.* We get out of life not what we put in, but what we are willing to allow in our lives. It flows through us, but it is not driven by us.

Yes, this program can be applied to any addictions, not just food, except that some of us need an intervention or to hit bottom to create an opening just to read this book. Most of us have more than one addiction, especially if we get rid of one only to replace its expression with another. I've seen food addicts who give up food

---

[2] *"Does Catholic praise for Mary Magdalene show progress towards women priests?" by By Trevor Timpson, BBC News, Jan. 12, 2017, http://www.bbc.com/news/uk-38528682.*

reach for smoking or shopping, for example. So, let's get to the heart of the matter and get started.

## WHAT IS THE DIVINE FEMININE?

When speaking of a "higher power," I usually use the word God or Goddess because it is most comfortable for me personally. If these words trigger you emotionally, feel free to use whatever word(s) works best for you.

God is neither male nor female, and paradoxically, God is both because I experience God as bigger than I experience all of that. Most religions believe that God cannot be defined at all. I can only share my personal experience. I used to try to find God in a book, but at the age of nineteen, I discovered that reading it repeatedly didn't create the personal relationship that I was looking for. That's why I call myself a mystic because I prefer to experience the Divine personally rather than intellectually.

In my heart, a love and light burns brightly. That is God within me. Around and outside me, God infuses all that is with the same light and love. God is in every cell of my physical being. God is the glue that holds the electrons to the atoms and binds my molecules together in the greatest wisdom. I choose to believe that God conspires with the rest of the universe to surprise and delight each of us every day. It is our job to notice and be grateful for such blessings—even when blessings come in the form of challenges. It is my work to listen to the divine light within me, and to follow that joyful inspiration with wisdom, ease and grace.

Having grown up in a Christian Pentecostal church, God was always described in the masculine. The God of the Old Testament could be judgmental, angry and quite a destructive father figure. He was strict about his laws and purportedly threw Adam and Eve out of the Garden, blaming Eve for wanting to eat from the Tree of Knowledge. Not wanting to be associated with such a seductress and "sinner," I grew up to value only masculine characteristics and never cultivated my feminine side. Our entire culture has done the same for a couple thousand years (patriarchy) creating a society that is very out of balance with itself and nature. Many pre-Christian societies revered the feminine and Her softer qualities. The patriarchy destroyed them.

All of our qualities are divine for they all come from the same God. I believe that all of our great religions are divinely inspired, for they all come from the same God originally. It is humanity—not God—that adds all the dogma over the years and makes the spiritual message sound different. The sun rises each morning— sometimes we call the day "Monday" the same sun rises again, and we call it "Tuesday" Similarly, God rises in different cultures at different times to offer wisdom for our human development. That's why different religions have different social teachings appropriate for their time and place. I still consider myself a Christian mystic, AND I get to enjoy the wisdom teachings of all religions. It would be silly to think that people who wake up on Monday are going to heaven, and people who wake up on Tuesday are going to hell. The God/Goddess I have come to know is bigger than that. I can easily create my own heaven or hell right here and now just by the stories I make up about what's happening.

However, you don't have to believe what I believe to make this system work for you. My intention is to offer the world of humanity more freedom to think for ourselves and ask —what is real?—rather than to answer that question with someone else's opinion or what a particular book may have to say. I believe it our responsibility to learn to discern what is real in our own feeling body. "Feeling navigation" is a required skill for spiritual development, particularly when we leave our bodies someday to become spirit again and need to navigate without our five physical senses (more about this later).

## MY STORY

After 35 years of developing my masculine qualities, I became a successful lawyer with my own law firm making a six-figure income and at the top of my intellectual game. I didn't have time for friends and didn't let my spouse contribute to me. I also found myself wondering why I didn't feel completely fulfilled and why I felt so exhausted all the time.

Men have much more testosterone than women have and their bodies use it to combat stress. Women must mostly rely on their adrenal glands. Mine were completely exhausted—my thyroid had to work harder so it soon became deplete. Finally, my own immune system started to attack my thyroid.

I also noticed at age 45 that many of my girlfriends began to have breast cancer. Breasts represent our feminine abundance and the gifts we bring, so many of which are not appreciated nor are they currently respected by many cultures. Sadly, breast cancer is on the rise and women are losing a symbol of their femininity to this disease.

On the larger scale, this masculine culture has been allowed to run rampant like a parasite on a host planet that is on a suicide mission. Without the balance of our feminine qualities, we have rewarded those who have conquered, dominated and controlled other humans (slavery) as well as the planet's resources unsustainably.

It is time for both men and women to embrace, cultivate and balance our masculine and feminine qualities if we are to survive as a species in harmony with our planet. This underlying imbalance feeds my addiction because lacking fulfillment, I find myself reaching to "fill up" on the feminine from sources outside myself—most often food. *When we remember that our desire to fill up is a spiritual one and we are unlimited spiritual beings, we realize we deserve to "have it all."* Finding tools to help us remember this is key because we are constantly bombarded by carefully crafted marketing to convince us that we need what they have to fill up our emptiness. Unless we fill that emptiness with self-generated joy, we will forever be dependent on eating, shopping, and external indulgences for little bits of joy in our lives. That's why **this program is about freedom.**

What if you could feel fulfilled right now, rather than "someday" when you lose 40 pounds, or when you have the "right" job, or find the "right" partner? What if you could simply generate the experience of joy—whenever you wanted—rather than wallowing in old stories of victimhood? If that were possible, you could *create a life you love regardless of your circumstances!*

## PUTTING THE STEPS INTO PRACTICE

To work the 13 steps, you will read one-step per week, broken down into daily bite-sized pieces. Each day has its own affirmation and action items. Speak the affirmation to yourself as often as you can remember, and if you like, print it on a card and tape it to your refrigerator each day. (Or purchase the *Affirmation Card Deck* available at www.DivingIntotheDivineFeminine.com)

Feel free to embellish and modify your process creating your own exercises as your intuition directs. The steps toward your healing are personal to YOU, and YOU are the expert. There is nothing to learn in this book, just reminders of what you already know.

1. Spiritual processes are not linear,
   but more like a spiral.

   Each of the 13 Steps builds on the last to some extent, so I recommend taking them in order the first time. As you move on to the next step, continue to practice the prior steps—do not abandon them. Do what you can, and move on to the next step each week regardless. We could work these steps endlessly and never be perfect. If a step feels incomplete, just plan to come back around to it for further development later. If it feels like you've already mastered a step, look to unwrap the next layer of unknown—a blind spot—it's like peeling an onion. Ask the universe to reveal it to you with grace and ease. Throughout this process, you are always have a choice. Therefore, YOU must give yourself the freedom to choose which exercises to attempt and which are not in alignment with your Self. I use the capital S in Self here because I want you to listen to your higher Self, the divinely connected Self. Listen to THAT Self.

2. Start a Journal.

Journal the answers to the following questions:

- *What would it take to accept myself and my addiction just as it is right now?*

- *Would I have to give something up?*

- *Am I willing, even though I may not know "how"?*

- *What do I get out of overeating or eating food that some-how sabotages my goals?*

If you're like me, you have lots of empty journals and don't want to write in any of them for fear that: 1) someone will later read it, and 2) it's too pretty to fill with my messy life notes. This is where the steps require you to step out of your comfort zone and just do it anyway in the face of those concerns. This is called courage. Trust the process in its imperfection. Don't have time? You must create time. **Add one-half hour to your calendar every day** so you have time to read the step and apply it to your life. Morning works best for me, but before bed is also a good time. Ideally, I do both.

3. Generate the feeling of well-being that comes from total acceptance . . .

. . . just as you are and just as you are not—with all of your "imperfections" including your addiction. Use the affirmation. "Fake it 'till you make it." How does it feel to stop making yourself "wrong"? How does it feel to love yourself regardless? YOU generate that feeling—it comes from telling yourself a different story. There's nothing wrong here! There's nothing to fix! Begin to notice when you don't feel "good," and what story you are telling yourself. Choose a different story that feels better. For example, most of my life, I retold the story "Something is wrong." I would find evidence for that everywhere because then I could be right about it. I could tell you what was wrong with my body (My hips are too big and don't fit in any pants.), in politics (corruption), in my relationships (He's not supportive enough.), in my closet (I don't have enough clothes.), in my bank account, etc., etc. When I realized that I was actually creating this story, I decided to choose a new one: "The entire universe is conspiring to surprise and delight me every day." Now I find evidence for that reality—and it's way more fun! I've become a magic moment collector. It doesn't matter if our story is "true" because we are limited in our personal perception of reality anyway. The stories we think are true are just limited thought patterns. Change the pattern and "voila"—a new reality that automatically creates new feelings.

For example, if two identical twin boys were given a shovel and told to clean up a horse's stall full of manure, they would have completely different experiences, depending on the story they make up about it. One boy might decide that he hates life because cleaning manure is a stinky, dirty job. The other boy might be excited to accomplish the same task because he thinks, "There must be a pony in here some-where!" The entire universe conspires to provide the pony when it hears this desire. Wouldn't YOU want to give a pony to this little boy?[i] That's why crowd funding has been so successful. We all want to conspire to manifest our dreams together.

## 4. Be Open to Miracles.

Our intelligence can often be our own worst enemy. The universe would shower us with abundance and every desire's fulfillment were it not for our limited thinking. Get out of the way! Notice when your own self-talk is stopping you. When someone embarks toward spiritual development such as these steps, there is no way to avoid the showering of Divine assistance that pours forth—sometimes in sur-prising ways. Ask for miracles then notice and be grateful for them.

## 5. Contribute.

Meaning and purpose, which is where happiness is most easily accessed, come from our ability to contribute to others. That is what will keep you coming back week after week. Your working the program 100% will inspire others, and their lives will change because of your example. You cannot contribute if you feel like you have nothing to give. You owe it to the world to complete this program for your-self, so you can help others heal in the future. That's right; once this program heals you, it doesn't end. This is not a one-way relationship. You must contribute back.

6. Share vulnerably.

Your courage to share vulnerably from your heart with at least one human being each week creates intimacy and connection—an important ingredient for your healing. It doesn't "look good" and may therefore feel scary to your ego. The more you hide, the more you feel isolated. The more you feel isolated, the more you want to eat. You are not alone! Set an example for others by having the courage to share vulnerably.

7. Declare your future.

Instead of focusing on the present moment and declaring what is so (Hi, I'm Heather, and I'm a food addict"), declare the future you want to live "into." It should truly inspire you. For example, you may declare a future of carefree delight, laughter and abundance. When generating your future, be careful that the words you choose are not a reaction against the past or even informed by the past, but rather the words are independently inspiring. For example, it is not as empowering to say "I am not a food addict" as it is to say, "I am powerful, free and beautiful." See the list of possible futures in Exhibit A to get you started.

# HOW POWERFUL PRACTICES WORK IN THIS PROGRAM

♥ **READ.** If you are approaching this program for the first time, read one of the 13 Steps each week in the order in which they appear. If you are returning to this program after completing all 13 Steps, feel free to go more deeply into any of the Steps that call you. Pay closest attention to the first three steps, which lay the foundation for the rest. Each step is then broken down into seven days. Each day, read the corresponding section.

♥ **AFFIRMATIONS.** Each day speak the affirmation aloud.

♥ **JOURNAL.** Take some time to journal about how this step applies to your life each day. This practice can include creating art, writing poetry, songs or modalities other than words.

♥ **EMBODY THE QUALITIES.** Each step has its own energetic qualities or archetypes. BECOME the energy of the Step. Generate it, feel it, and cultivate the qualities. If I were my own Great Mother, for example, I might close my eyes to feel completely and totally loved within my own skin. BEING the Great Mother is bigger than my personality, it is a mythic persona. You may be tapping into a part of your Higher Self that have not met before. Try it out.

♥ **TAKE ACTION.** From this state of BEing, listen to your inspiration bubbling up so that you will know what action steps would be in alignment with your new way of being. Make a list. For example, in Step 1, I might feel inspired to take a warm bath or cook a healthy dinner because that seems like I'm being a Great Mother to myself. If I really let myself BE in my feminine, however, I might instead feel inspired to receive a warm bath and enjoy a healthy dinner prepared by a friend or lover. My initial approach is more masculine by directly making things happen by doing them myself, and the second approach is more feminine by receiving. Both approaches are valid, but I've spent my whole life making things happen from my masculine self, which leaves me physically exhausted. Our entire culture is yang—masculine—focused. This program encourages us to balance that out with a lot more yin—feminine. What would it be like to ask for help and let yourself receive?

♥ **CALENDAR** when you plan to complete your homework. If it's not on my calendar, it generally doesn't happen until it becomes a habit.

♥ **BONUS POINTS.** Everything else that looks like homework or exercises in this book or on our website is just gravy! Do them as bonus points if you feel inspired and your support team will applaud you, not to mention what YOU might get out of it. In school, I played down my intelligence so others wouldn't think I was showing off. In contrast, here we are playing BIG and supporting each other in pushing the envelope on freedom and self-expression. This is NOT a competition; it's a garden of delight where we celebrate each other's victories and breakthroughs.

# HOW DO YOU RELATE TO HOMEWORK?

People have different relationships to homework. Becoming more aware of your own resistance may help you find your growth edge Here are five kinds of reactions to homework:

1.  *"I am only as valuable as what I accomplish."*

    For twenty-four years, I went to school and did homework, not really to learn anything, but to pass the test, get good grades, get into college so I could get a good job, buy a house and be happy. If I didn't do my homework, I felt bad about myself. If I got good grades, I felt good about myself. I made it mean something.

    This program offers homework as a gift, not something on which to judge your success or failure. If you usually judge yourself harshly, it's time to give up that story—it just doesn't work because your accomplishment or lack thereof does not define you. There is nothing you could do or not do, that would make you any more perfect and divine than you already are. There is nothing wrong and nothing to fix. Do you love your children more or less based on their homework? Of course not, but you may want them to do their homework so they can manifest their dreams. Apply the same logic to yourself.

2.  *"I must work hard."*

    My old limited thought pattern said, "The harder I work these steps, the more I'll get out of them and the closer to freedom from addiction I will be." In which case, I may just get addicted to the 13 Step Program and accomplish nothing. How sneaky of my old self!

I often have to remind myself that enlightenment can happen in a moment of grace for people who have never sought it. Enlightenment can also bypass someone who read every self-help book ever published. For me, enlightenment would be clear and complete freedom from all addiction, as though a veil had been lifted. This is my intention. You don't have to work for it or earn it—it can be effortless. Be open to the possibility that the light may turn on at any moment in the dark room and reveal all. Perhaps a few sparks happen each day until together they form a pattern of awareness that you never noticed before. It is your job to notice!

Be in awe and wonder of how the universe is rooting for you and giving you clues all the time. It's your job to collect them. If ALL you did were follow the homework to the letter, as an intellectual experiment, you would gain more knowledge, but not more freedom. Your freedom includes breaking OUT of the limited homework to find your own exercises that work best for you.

3. *"I don't do homework."*

There are those of us who did not do well in school and resisted other people telling us what to do, for whom the idea of "homework" will repel us instantly. If you usually rebel against homework, now is an opportunity to "surrender." You always have a choice in this program because this program is about freedom! This program is here to empower you, not make you feel victimized by homework.

4.  *"Tell me what to do."*

For those who excel in the linear world and prefer to be told what to do step-by-step, homework may feel like a flotation device in the middle of the stormy sea. Structure is a wonderful gift, until it is too small for your Mythic Self, then it becomes a golden cage. As you do the homework, start to notice if it's working for you. What is it that's missing in the homework? What do you want more of in the homework? If you designed the homework section, how would it be different? Now do THAT homework. Homework should never stifle your own expertise and magnificence. Stop playing small.

5.  *"I don't want to do the homework."*

Homework in this program has no value in itself. It is the intention of the homework that matters. WHY do you do your homework? Make a list of what you intend to get out of this program. For me, my intention is freedom, love, and connection. I am also tired of suffering and watching others suffer. I now choose vibrant health.

# STEP 1:

. . . . . . . . . . . . . . . . . . .

# Surrender

# Day 1:

Surrender to Things Just As They
Are and Just As They're Not

## AFFIRMATION:

*"I hereby accept and love myself just the way I am, and the way I am not. I surrender and accept my experience. I am whole and complete, precious and lovable. I am perfect RIGHT NOW where I am in the process."*

From a larger spiritual perspective, this is all true, but for most of us, this declaration sounds crazy, because a part of us knows that when addiction runs our lives, it is not our natural state of being. We know it is a disease and not something to "accept." Rather, it is something that is not an authentic expression of our higher Self, and which impedes our ability to accomplish our purpose on this planet.

# WHAT YOU RESIST PERSISTS!

Regardless, do not resist where you are in your process right now—even hitting bottom has its purpose. Let's assume that your soul is so wise that it chose addiction, as its teacher— and that you're here to learn from addiction or any other suffering you have chosen as your companion in this lifetime. Let's assume that you are far more powerful than you may realize, and that you have somehow chosen your current addiction and all of the circumstances of your life on a subconscious level. In this step, you are being asked to choose them on a conscious level.

Just as we surrender to our third grade teacher who says we have to learn math, we will honor our addiction as one of our greatest teachers. Once we learn the lessons of addiction, we won't need it anymore, and we will graduate. This program is one of discovery! Often is it is our greatest suffering that becomes our greatest pearl of wisdom. Just like oysters turn a grain of irritating sand into its most beautiful treasure. We can't take treasure with us when we graduate from this lifetime, but we CAN take our experiences and spiritual treasure.

If you find yourself resisting any exercise, just notice what the objection is, thank your ego mind for sharing, and do the exercise anyway. For example, you might think, "that's not true." It doesn't matter if the affirmation or exercise is true or not. What matters is whether it works. Let this be your new test for the stories you tell. Ask yourself "How is that story working for me?" For example, we often make wishes on our candles at a birthday party. It may not be "true" that blowing out candles makes wishes come true, but it seems to "work for us," because it creates a feeling of expansion and happiness.  Go with it to find out what, if anything, the exercise reveals to you.

Our linear minds are often trapped in a dualistic conversation that says, "That's right" or "wrong," "That's true" or "untrue," "I agree," or "I disagree."  If you allow these mental judgments to stop you, you will dramatically limit your experience in this life, which is mostly GRAY, not black and white at all.

"Between the concept of right and wrong, there is a field.  I will meet you there."[ii]

# Day 2:

## Feeling Depleted?
## Surrender to Nourishment

## AFFIRMATION:

*"I choose nourishment. I choose to connect with my higher power. I am filled. I am fulfilled. I have always been embraced and loved unconditionally."*

This archetype of the Great Mother is about nourishing myself. How can I trust so deeply that I don't need to fill my "empty" void? How can I appreciate the emptiness like a golden chalice—the Holy Grail—that has been prepared so that I am consciously filled with the gifts of the spirit—whether they come in the form of food, music, uplifting movies, emotional intimacy with others, art, conscious touch, kindness, inspiration or fulfilling my dreams.

No wonder we eat so much—we're so hungry for so much more than just food, but in our culture we have forgotten to fill up on what we really desire—thinking that if we just have more stuff, we'll feel better.

## PUTTING THIS INTO PRACTICE

How can I create more sanctuary, rest and retreat for myself? I can set aside the time every day to nourish my soul. I create a sacred place to sit and BE. This is a place to empty myself so that I may be filled with something other than food. It requires that I drop OUT of my head away from too much thinking and into my feeling space, my heart and OPEN. I shall fill up on remembering how grateful I am for all that I have been given thus far, for all the beauty of my life, and for all the love, people, and blessings. I shall listen to beautiful music, inspirational writing—like mystical poetry—enjoy images that inspire me to decorate a sacred place or altar that honors my beliefs. I shall give myself plenty of time (at least one-half hour) every day to feed my soul.

I choose nourishing thoughts and feelings. If a thought or feeling depletes me, I choose a different one. I have a wonderful list of affirmations that light me up. I even have a set of inspirational cards that I made so I can choose one at random every morning and place it on my sacred space like an intention for my day.

This is NOT the time to do a cleanse. This is the time to nourish myself. For me, that means hot lentil soups, cooked green vegetables, bone-broth, protein smoothies with cinnamon and ginger tea. I've learned this because I have a nutrition coach/chiropractor, an acupuncturist, a massage therapist and a naturopathic doctor who all agree and I feel better when I eat this way. I also know that walnuts and inositol magically stabilize my blood sugar and release me from white-knuckle sugar cravings. I am not on a diet—that sounds like scarcity and limitation—I am giving myself the super food nutrition that I need and deserve to honor my beautiful body. There is nothing "good" or "bad" to eat. Everything wants to nourish me in some way; even chocolate cake nourishes my little girl's desire to have a treat.

However, if a food depletes me—I choose not to eat it. For example, soda pop depletes the calcium out of my bones. Since it's not a whole food and doesn't bring its own minerals for digestion, my body has to supply them, depleting them from other places where they are needed. When I eat depleting food, it makes me crave even more food. I want nourishing minerals in my body!

I choose to schedule time to go grocery shopping and prepare nourishing food—like a fun game that I get to play. This breaks me out of my comfort zone and old habits. The game is to come up with both a delicious and a healthy food plan. It's time for abundance thinking—not scarcity thinking. Avocados and whole foods beautifully prepared are in order! If I don't have time to cook, I'll ask someone to cook for me or have the food delivered. I'll start my day with hot lemon water or fresh celery juice to reset my PH, followed by a high quality breakfast.

## POWERFUL PRACTICE

Determine what your body and soul need for nourishment and make a list. Enlist whatever support you need to make sure you are nourished. For example, add self-care items to your calendar to make sure they happen—exercise, etc.[i]

# Day 3:

## Surrender to the Unknown

## AFFIRMATION:

*"I surrender to what I don't know and what I don't know I don't know. I trust in the vast unknown to hold me. All is well."*

One of my earliest fears was trusting that everything was going to be all right because I didn't know the future. I ate anxiously often wanting something in my mouth (usually potato chips) to numb my fear. I got anxious about money, relationships, politics, and the global suffering I saw on TV every day. The media feeds on our fears and anxieties. Sometimes in my fear of the unknown, I would act out familiar habits of eating even though I knew better. Intellectually, I knew the processed foods will make me feel worse, but I ate them anyway.

The three things I do to break free from my fear or lack of trust are:

1. Trust. I CHOOSE to believe that life is great, that we can ALL have it ALL, and that everything happens for a reason promoting our spiritual development. In short, I have to remind myself that everything is going to be OK. It doesn't matter whether our beliefs are actually true or not. The measure of a useful belief can be found in the results it produces. In this case, my belief creates peace and joy rather than fear. Try this on today.

2. To take 100% responsibility for my life. If I CHOOSE to believe that everything occurs in my life because I've chosen it, then that means I can create something different at any moment. That is powerful and leaves me inspired to create my future rather than feel powerless about my circumstances. Try this on today.

3. To drop into meditation and remember my spiritual essence. I'll share more about this in Step 3.

# Day 4:

· · · · · · · · · · · · · · · · ·

## Surrender to Receptivity

## AFFIRMATION:

*"I receive."*

Assume today that the entire universe is conspiring to support you. Assume that your only job is to notice this phenomenon, receive the gifts and be grateful for them. Try not to have preconceived ideas about what that support might look like because that might get in your way. Just be open minded, open hearted and open to support.

I dreamed once that I was in a small dark shack in the rain forest in Puget Sound, Washington. There were a few leaky holes in the roof and I ran around frantically catching a drop or two in each of my seven golden chalices. I worked quickly moving them around continually inside the shack hoping for a little water. All I had to do was step outside the mildewed shack and stand in the rain to have abundant water filling all my chalices without any effort. That's as simple as this step is. Identify how you might move out of the limitations of your mind and how you would be open to what receptivity would look like for you.

I learned at age 3 when my father left us to "do it myself"—our individualistic western culture promotes this idea. I spent the first 35 years of my life in this mode and only recently allowed a partner (in my case, a man) to contribute to me. That receptivity required me to surrender and trust him. Let yourself lean on someone stable this week. Practice asking for help. Don't limit yourself to this 3-dimensional-plane, but ask your angels, fairies, ancestors, guides, dreams and higher powers to assist you now.

It is divinely feminine to receive. How can you be more receptive?

# Day 5:

................

## Surrender to Your Magnificence

### AFFIRMATION:

*"I am a magnificent being, much bigger than I ever thought possible. I'm amazing, full of surprises, and so is everyone else. I now step fully into my magnificence, embodying my Divine essence."*

Believe it or not, this may take a lot of courage. One of our greatest fears is not that we are inadequate, but that we are magnificent beyond our imagination.

We are trained to play small. I have wanted connection, amongst women, and I have been afraid to express fully my beauty for fear of female competitiveness. I thought I needed to gain weight so that other women would like me and not see me as competition. Sometimes I gained weight to avoid unwanted sexual attention from men. That's playing small too.

Now it's time to celebrate our magnificence. What are you most amazing qualities? What keeps you from expressing them? What would you look like if you played big? Begin to create a vision board of your magnificent Self.

# FAKE IT TILL YOU MAKE IT

Now it's actually time to BE who you really are. At first, this may feel fake. You'll get over it! It really took me about a year to own my big beautiful Divine Feminine Self. In the meantime, I pretended. I started to dress like my magnificent Self, decorated my room magnificently and created my life with more freedom and flair. I would ask, "What would I eat if I were a Goddess?" "What car would I drive?" "Where would I live?"

Warning: The world is longing for the Divine Feminine to reemerge. Others may begin to see you this way and want to worship you. I choose to graciously allow this, but not for my ego's sake, just in service. Think of what it might be like to be Amma, appearing to be a saint and hugging everyone in the world. She got used to it. You will too. Graciously receive the gifts and adoration that come in response to this practice.

# Day 6:

Surrender to New Eating Habits

## AFFIRMATION:

*"I am willing to take whatever steps are necessary to create a wonderful relationship with food."*

I used to hate food, wishing I didn't have to eat it ever again. That would be so much easier than facing my addiction every morning. When I transitioned from being a stressed-out lawyer for twenty years to living my dream in Hawaii as a mermaid, I assumed that food addiction would just magically disappear. I assumed that the stress of being a lawyer was to blame. However, as a wise person once said to me, "Wherever you are, there you are!"

To heal food addiction, we will actually have to create new eating habits. This will require a WILLINGNESS to change as well as some effort. It doesn't have to be "hard" and you don't have to know how to do that yet, but you must answer the following question with a yes to get started: Are you willing to change the way you eat?

If not, then you may not be in touch with WHY you want to heal from food addiction. Knowing the why is critical to your recovery. Make a list of all the things you want to do and be in this lifetime. Circle the ones that are the most important to you. Ask yourself, if I suffer from food addiction, will I be able to do or be these important things?

If you are still not willing, then you are a functional addict, just as I used to be, and you haven't hit bottom yet. No worries—hitting bottom will be your motivation in the near future. Spirit always has a way of getting our attention when it's time for us to grow. I prefer an easier route—willingness before I hit bottom. I visualize what bottom would look like for me—write it in my journal and pretend it has already happened.

If you ARE willing, begin to make a list of what foods you already know work well for your body and what foods don't. Over the next 12 months, continue to explore this and add them to your list so you don't forget when you are hungry.

Are you willing to give up old ideas and beliefs about food? Be open-minded to the possibility that your old ideas and beliefs may not be working for you. Are you willing to surrender your ideas of how long it should take to heal or what your ideal body weight should be? It is enough at first to be willing. You don't have to figure out "how." The how will reveal itself soon enough.

# Day 7:

......................

## Surrender to Feelings

## AFFIRMATION:

*"I am responsible for my emotions and the stories I make up that cause them. I choose to own them or rewrite them powerfully."*

When I eat to numb my feelings, they are packed into my fat cells for later processing. That's like eating on a credit card, and I'll have to pay the price later by dealing with the emotions when they come up. They come up when that fat cell releases the old emotion or trauma back into my system as it leaves my body.

Hopefully I'm drinking plenty of water to help this process occur gracefully. I hope that I have created space on my calendar to process my old feelings! This can be time to journal about them (see Exhibit H). It can be taking a bath once a week to have a good cry. It can be date night to discuss feelings with friends and loved ones. The faster we process the old feelings, the faster we lose the need to cover them up. Ask yourself, "What am I most upset about?"

or "What do I want others not to know about me?" This can be the hardest part of the process for some of us after decades of cover up.

This is not an excuse to dump things on others, however. You are 100% responsible for your emotional reactions and the triggers that create them. Our emotions are often a reaction to a story we made up about reality. Unpack your emotions to get to the underlying story that now pretends to be more than just a story—it feels REAL. This is an illusion. We make up stories all the time and then convince ourselves that they're real.

We create our reality this way and call it our past. Our past then becomes our future only because we recreate the same story repeatedly with different players and circumstances. We are stuck in a cycle of storytelling. Ask yourself, "How is that story working for me?" Does it make me happy, feel loved and create more love for others?" If your answer is no, then make up a new story.

Once you surrender your attachment to the old story, you can easily make up a new one that works better for the future you desire to create, since we just make everything up anyway. If there is a TRUTH out there, only our higher power has the ability to see all perspectives on it. Therefore, understanding that our vision as humans is quite limited in its perception helps us give up the idea that we have to be "right."

For example, I always used to think, "Something was wrong." I spent my whole life looking for evidence of that. This didn't work well for me because I lived in a world with little trust and little appreciation of what was going well.

If you are willing to give up being "right" and more interested in creating a story that works for YOU, you will be free to create whatever you desire regardless of the circumstances.

You can identify stories that aren't working for you by asking yourself what makes you feel resigned, cynical, powerless or judgmental. Use your journal to rewrite at least one disempowering story you tell yourself. At first, it will pretend to be REAL and refuse to be called just a "story."

If you are stuck, it may be because some things that happen are real. If my friend said, "You look fat in those pants." The fact that she said those words is real, but the story I make up about it later, like "She's a jerk. She said that on purpose to make me feel bad" is not real. It's just my story about what happened.

Distinguishing what happened from my story is key and not as easy as it sounds when emotions run high. What's worse is that our friends and families agree with our stories and make them even more real. You might begin to notice when you do this for others and when they do it for you thinking loyalty in storytelling is a kindness. It's actually a conspiracy and has nothing to do with reality. So, if we make up stories all day long, please make up stories that work for the life you want to create!

# STEP 2:

.....................

*Compassion*

Compassion is generated in our heart space. In this step, where we remember how to get out of "thinking about things," we drop down into our bodies, specifically into our hearts, and use "feeling navigation." Compassion is a state of BEING, not a DOING, although compassionate action naturally flows from this state of being.

For most of my life, I avoided spending time in my heart for several reasons. I share these ideas assuming that I'm not alone and my naming them may be helpful to others:

1.  *Humans are wired to be empathic.* We can feel the pain and ecstasy of others. Some of us are very sensitive to this gift and eat food to numb out when upset surrounds us. Mashed potatoes seem to do the trick for me. Without psychic boundaries, we often feel depleted around other people. Until recently, no one taught me how to create energetic boundaries with others, the television news or other over-stimulating sources of toxic energy.

2.  As a lawyer, *I was paid to stay in my head.* I didn't even think about the rest of my body most of the time. I lived from my neck up and felt that my body's needs were a distraction. Most lawyers I knew were hardened just to survive. I played that game at first and went to battle every day in the court-room, but I didn't like what I saw and didn't enjoy being a warrior. I wanted to stay soft. I wanted to be real and trust-worthy. I had to create my own law firm, choose my clients carefully and focus on keeping everyone out of the court-room to accomplish that.

3.  I felt that *how much I accomplished established my worth.* Merely being was "not enough." I believed my resume documented my self-worth.

4.  *Western culture* applauded my driven work ethic. I spent 24 years in school training my mind to do things like math and logic. Not once did anyone offer a class in compassion.

5.  My religion taught me to read the holy writings intellectually, looking to understand God through the words of a book. I thought the more I read the book, the closer to God I would be. I did not realize until I was almost twenty years old that I had to get out of my head and into my heart to *experience the Divine directly and mystically.* Reading about relationships didn't cut it.

Stop reading this book now and just "drop in" to your heart space. Generate within yourself a feeling of compassion for something you care about or someone. What does it feel like? Compassion is unconditional love, regardless of the circumstances. Now, experience this feeling about yourself. Next, feel compassion for someone you consider an enemy. Was it difficult to generate these feelings? Allowing compassion to flow through us may take some practice if we've been taught not to value it most of our lives.

# Day 1:

. . . . . . . . . . . . . . . . . .

## Forgiveness

### AFFIRMATION:

*"I am sorry. Please forgive me. Thank you. I love you. "*

The past has a way of recreating itself in our future. So, if you want more of the past, do nothing. If you want a different future and are genuinely committed to freedom, then it is time to forgive everyone and everything that has ever happened since the beginning of the beginning. This is a radical shift for most of us. We have this capacity because we have the Divine within us, and the Divine does this all day long with a radiant heart. The irony of this action, from the Divine's perspective, is that there is nothing to forgive. When we step back and use our bird's eye view, we see all that is. We know that all of us are collectively in spiritual evolution, learning our soul lessons and that nothing is an accident or a mistake. Our daily choices are merely growth opportunities. This human experience is a classroom for our spiritual development.

If you were watching your child walk for the first time and your child stumbled, would you judge your child harshly? No, you would see stumbling as a critical part of learning to walk. You would not say, "This child is defective because she can't understand calculus at age 3." You would see your child as divine and perfect in her current state of development. This is divine clarity.

For myself, I began to see my lifelong struggle with food as a gift. My food dependency has taught me compassion for others who struggle. It has shown me kindness and generosity. It has taught me the value of self-love and reflection. To reclaim my power and freedom, it has forced me to seek a deeper relationship with the spiritual Divine and with Self-love. I came for these treasures, and now that I have discovered them, I can choose to develop spiritually without the suffering. I can make a different choice.

Now is the time to forgive all actions in the past, present, and future, for all beings and all ages. Stop reading now and DO IT, speak it, write it. It might take a while to get it all out. It might come with tears and anger. You might bump into resistance. Just keep going!

Today's affirmation is a very powerful prayer from the Hawaiian tradition of Ho'oponopono, meaning to make something right.[iii] Say this affirmation repeatedly all day about everything. Let's assume that I am responsible for everything in my world, and from this powerful stance, I can be forgiven and heal the world. I find it particularly helpful when I watch the news because I used to feel powerless to do anything about all the suffering. Now, with this one powerful prayer, I can request a change in the current state of affairs through forgiveness of whatever role I play in creating more suffering in this world. The prayer asks for Divine intervention, and the "thank you" releases it, as if it is done.

Forgiveness is possibly the most powerful thing we can do to create real freedom for others and ourselves.

Here in Kona, Hawaii, where I live, we have an ancient city dedicated to this concept. This place is the City of Refuge (Pu'uhonua O Honaunau). If you broke the law in ancient times, you could be forgiven entirely by escaping to the City of Refuge before you were arrested. Create such a city in your heart for yourself and all beings.

# Day 2:

. . . . . . . . . . . . . . . . . .

## Boundaries

## AFFIRMATION:

*"I am an expert at saying "no" with grace and ease. I create clear boundaries."*

It's time to practice saying "no." Fierce boundaries are an important aspect of compassion for self and others. Saying "no" to one thing is also saying "yes" to another. For example, if I say "no" to a friend who asks me to go to breakfast, I'm saying "yes" to honoring the self-care time I've set aside in the mornings. If I say "no" to purchasing another trinket, I'm saying "yes" to the freedom from having to store it and "yes" to working less just to keep up with my old spending patterns.

My old story was that I didn't want to hurt someone's feelings so I would say "yes" and then resent that decision later on. I used to keep myself poor so that I would have an excuse to say "no" when people asked me for money. I used to keep my schedule overfull so I would have an excuse to say "no" when people wanted me to spend time with them. Now, I choose to let people be responsible for their own feelings and reactions when I say, "I can't take time for lunch right now because I'm spending all my extra time on self-care and rest at this moment."

Write down where you need clearer boundaries. Do you need to remove food in the house for self-care? Do you need a boundary to allow more time and space for meditation and exercise? Do you need more space in your relationships? Many people continue to allow themselves to live in toxic or unsafe environments. You are the captain of your own ship and the keeper of your schedule. Update your living arrangements, pantry, and your calendar to include the boundaries you need. Make a list of what those changes would look like and take action.

# Day 3:

. . . . . . . . . . . . . . . . . .

## Atonement

## AFFIRMATION:

*"I choose to take the powerful position that I am 100% responsible for how the world occurs in and around me. I courageously make amends to free myself and others from the past."*

It is time to make amends for any injury we may have created. The trick here is to take 100% responsibility for whatever is not working in your life WITHOUT making yourself wrong. That's why we started with forgiveness! To identify why atonement is necessary, listen for where in your life you are feeling stuck, hopeless or cynical. Consider that YOU may be creating this experience in your life for some unconscious payoff. I know how radical that can sound when we've spent years blaming our circumstances. This is an exercise in turning that story on its head. Go with me for a moment and be curious. In the past, my payoff usually involved me being "right" or not having to be responsible for something. Sometimes my payoff was the ability to dominate or manipulate someone to get my way.

Taking responsibility is powerful because then YOU have the power to clean it up. It doesn't matter If It doesn't seem "true" that you are responsible. Taking responsibility is a choice (not a reflection of reality). For example, many of us blame our parents for lack of parenting the way we wanted it to happen. What if before we were even born, we chose our parents? What if this choice allowed us to learn something from their challenging circumstances?

Let's try on atonement in your life now. *First, identify where you may have caused someone harm.* For example, I wasn't talking to my sister much because I was judging her and making her wrong all the time. I blamed HER. To atone for this, I first had to *identify the story I had made up* about her so I could name it. I then had to **own what I was getting out of it,** which was that I was able to feel right and superior to her. Then I had to **get in touch with the cost** to me sadness from the loss of connection and love with her. By getting in touch, I mean really feel it. If tears come next, you've arrived. Now, in touch with my heart and feeling body, I create a new future vision for my relationship with my sister, i.e., love, connection, fun, mutual support, etc. From THIS place, I could pick up the phone and say, "I'm sorry, I've been a jerk, and have been blaming YOU for our not talking lately. I've been making you wrong to feel better about myself. I miss you. I miss being able to pick up the phone and connect with you. I really want that with you again, and I love you. Can you forgive me?"[2]

Our lives only work as well as our relationships with others. Everything is at stake here. Start with the hardest atonement first, and then the rest will feel easy to you. Don't save the hardest to last, thinking you should practice more. You must be vulnerable and

---

[2] *I learned this approach to cleaning up the past at the Forum of Landmark Education, which I can't recommend strongly enough. (landmarkworldwide.com)*

ready to hear how much pain you may have caused another without beating yourself up about it and without resisting it, whether their perception is "true" or not. Simply breathe, forgive yourself, and stay soft. It is more important to have a connection with others than to be "right" all the time. Choose to give up whatever stops you from atonement in all areas of your life. Don't forget your relationship with food, money, religion, and politics. This process can take time, so take on just one atonement per day for as long as it takes.

The most potent act of atonement I have ever witnessed was by a woman whose father had molested and abused her as a child. She hadn't spoken to him in about twenty years. She freed herself from the victim-story of blame and shame. She stopped judging him for the past. In the end, she powerfully created a safe relationship with him. She has invited her father back into her life because she wants her father in her life, on her terms, this time as an adult with clear boundaries.

The ego, feeling too vulnerable, doesn't like this step and usually resists STRONGLY. *Cleaning up your past is how you can be truly free.* Use your support group and buddy system if you need courage.

You don't always have to involve the harmed parties in your atonement process—particularly if they've already passed over. Sometimes it could do more harm than good to tell an ex-spouse that you acted unfaithfully for many years. In that case, you might write a letter instead and burn it in the end, rather than deliver it. Use wisdom here, because, on the other hand, it may be freeing for your ex-spouse to hear what he/she probably already suspected.

Atonement may require more than just words. You may need to pay a debt, for example. You might find out what the harmed party needs to heal.

Do not fall into the pitfall of guilt. Taking full responsibility for everything that occurs in your life does not mean you should consider yourself wrong for it. You are in your own process of spiritual and emotional development, and you will create realities of "contrast" just to know what more you don't want. Like children, sometimes we try what doesn't work to find out what does work. That's life, and it's a gift.

# Day 4:

· · · · · · · · · · · · · · · · · · ·

## Connecting to Source

## AFFIRMATION:

*"I find all the love I need at the Source."*

By looking for love outside of myself—whether in another person or in food—I will never find what I'm really looking for. All the love I seek is in the Source, the Divine love, which exists within all things—including me. If the Divine is like the ocean, then I am a drop of water in that ocean made in his/her image and holding a hologram of the infinite. We all can generate more love than our bodies can ever hold. When I look for these qualities outside myself, I end up trying to fill a hungry black hole with the wrong kind of food. It feels hopeless. Stop relying on others to meet your needs—create some room in your relationships to remember that YOU are already whole and complete. You are directly connected to Source, and if you don't feel completely loved and content, then you can choose to generate those feelings now.

What if instead, there's nothing wrong and nothing to fix? Let that sink in. How does that feel? From this vantage point, what would you eat? What would you wear? What would you "do"? Who would be your friends? Standing in your wholeness, how would your world respond to you differently? How would your body react?

# Day 5:

. . . . . . . . . . . . . . . . . .

## Healing my Wounded Child

## AFFIRMATION:

*"I am not my mind. I am not my body. I am not my thoughts. I am not my emotions. I am simply love."*

Our most profound compassion usually comes from our deepest suffering. Each of us endured a childhood crisis. If you don't remember one, let me remind you. One occurred at the moment you made up the story that you were "separate" from all others. Since each of us came into this world from unity consciousness, which is an accurate reality from a spiritual perspective, this was a crisis in identity! At that moment, you left the 'Garden of Eden.' Most of us continued to make up stories after that to "survive."

In my life, I decided I had to take care of myself and everyone else since that fatherly role went missing in my life at age three. I've been independent and overly responsible ever since. This affected my eating habits because I felt that food was scarce, and I became the youngest entrepreneur to buy it for us. I also began to hoard it. I secretly kept a box of penny candy under my bed. Since sugar was not allowed in my home, this box was my rebellion and my expression of control.

It is not enough to know my child's wounds; I must also identify how that three-year-old continued to drive my life and my eating habits. Finally, I had to embrace my three-year-old's fear of "not enough" food, resentment for father's absence, and my child's desire to be in control. I hated to face it, but it was time for me to grow up! It was time for me both to love and listen to the whinings of my little three-year-old AND to run my life from my Higher Self, from the larger divine plan. It is much easier to give up the foods that don't serve me if I give my three-year-old what she REALLY wanted in the first place—love. I do that by listening to her concerns and fears, and then lovingly reassuring her that the old stories aren't real, that WE make-up the stories. I explain to her that *in reality, everyone is NOT separate; we just appear to be so for a short time, like waves on the ocean.* In a spiritual sense, everything is going to be all right because disease and death do not touch our souls. We are just here for the joy and the lessons of being in a human form for a time.

Journal about your inner child's wounding, about how it still runs your life, and how you might offer the love your child desires. Whenever we are touching the subconscious, we are reaching the core of our eating habits. If our habits were conscious, we could see and deal with them. It's time to dive deep.

# Day 6:

. . . . . . . . . . . . . . . . . .

## Compassion for the Chemistry of Compulsive Eating

## AFFIRMATION:

*"I am powerful over food and make my own decisions."*

Understanding intellectually WHY it can feel so difficult to put the bag of potato chips down can help to create compassion for ourselves. Most of my self-loathing in the past came from self-judgment. My story was that a "lack of discipline" caused my compulsive eating. If instead of creating a story, we realize that eating healthy may take an act of spiritual victory over our chemistry, then compassion instead of judgment may emerge from us. If I eat from self-loathing, I hopelessly keep eating the bag of potato chips. If I eat from compassion, I tend to ask, "What am I REALLY hungry for?"

Most of the processed food in the grocery store is filled with preservatives and other chemicals disguised as nutrition. Marketing for foods plays on our emotions and makes us want to it. Eating foods, which are not nutritious, only make us crave them more. The movie "Sugar Coated"[iv] makes it very clear that the sugar industry has created an entire nation of sugar addicts using the same tactics as the tobacco industry. If sugar is your addiction, then this movie is a must see. Sugar is added to almost every food we buy. Sugar is a poison and like heroin, keeps us coming back. There is a chemical component to our compulsion, and a multimillion-dollar conspiracy to keep us addicted.

Additionally, the same industry has used marketing to create an emotional culture around sugar that it equals love and family. Imagine Christmas without sugar! How could you go to a birthday party and not eat the cake and frosting? It's now a cultural tradition to fill up on sugar at Halloween and in our Easter baskets, not to mention chocolates on Valentine's Day. This is not a mere coincidence. Sugar is sold as the glue that makes life sweet. It will take some effort on our part now to unwind our holidays from sugar and replace our traditions with meaningful gifts.

My history includes a lifetime of chronic yeast infections and constipation—these are related to me. After colon hydrotherapy (a colon cleanse), the sugar cravings and mental fog lift like a veil, and I am free for a moment of clarity. When I'm constipated, it feels as though a sugar craving entity possess me. Chemically speaking, this is correct, but not just one entity, millions of them—yeast that reproduces in a sluggish colon.

As I write this chapter, I've been "off" sugar for 4 weeks, and I have to say, it's truly a miracle. The only way I will sustainably stay "sober" from my drug of choice (sugar), is to be vigilant about my self-care, particularly by remembering WHO I really am, spiritually speaking, and embodying my Divine essence. When it comes to saying "no" to sugar, I need my fierce compassion to create healthy boundaries (almost warrior-like). In the Divine Feminine world, I like to feel as though I'm Durga, the Hindu Goddess who rode a lion and wielded an invincible sword against corruption. The latest Wonder Woman[v] movie may be more comfortable for Western Culture to relate to as an archetype.

Journal about the ways you judge yourself for food addiction and explore how you could be more compassionate with yourself.

# Day 7:

## Feel Your Feelings...All of them

### AFFIRMATION:

*"I have courage to feel my feelings and love myself unconditionally."*

Imagine how it might feel for a mother to hold her only new-born child. Now, hold your feelings like that.

When I eat to numb my feelings, the "food is packed" into my fat cells for later processing. That means I've been eating on a credit card and I'll have to pay the price later, with interest. These emotions can return when that fat cell releases into my system as it leaves my body. Hopefully, I'm drinking plenty of water to help this process occur gracefully. Also, I need to have created space on my calendar to process my old feelings! This can be a good time to journal about them. Other ways to process the emotions can be taking a bath once a week to have a good cry or having a date night to discuss feelings with friends and loved ones. The faster we process the old feelings, the faster we lose the need to cover them up. Ask, "What am I most upset about," or "What do I want others not to know about me"? This can be the hardest part of the process for some of us (me particularly) after decades of cover-up.

# TOOLS

1. ## Try Hypnosis.

   A good hypnotist can take you right to the stories in your unconscious, and help you rewrite them from an adult perspective to bring them back to consciousness. One hypnosis session kept me sugar-free for 4 months WITHOUT EFFORT.

2. ## Use Spiritual Bathing.

   It is a powerful tool for forgiveness. Create a sacred space that includes a bath or pool of water. Saltwater is particularly healing. Wash away all that does not serve you. Welcome any tears and let them flow to wash away what is on the inside.

3. ## Read stories or watch inspiring films

   Read stories or watch inspiring films of compassionate heroes such as Quan Yin, Mahatma Gandhi, Christ, Saint Francis of Assisi.

4. ## Embody the Goddess of Compassion.

   Step into Her shoes for a moment—be that part of yourself that is bigger than your personality—and be the Divine Feminine aspect of your Self.

5. Surround yourself with soothing colors and smells

   ...such as lavender. Amethyst crystal is also your ally.

6. Soften more.

7. Practice clear boundaries.

# STEP 3:

· · · · · · · · · · · · · · · · · ·

*Know Thy Self*

Addiction or giving our power away to food *begins* as a spiritual amnesia, a forgetfulness of **who we really are** and how to truly fill up our spiritual gas tank. So instead, we try to fill it up with food or sugar. This is not to say that there isn't a powerful physical and emotional component, but they are not the *original* source of the core issue. Let's focus on the source first.

# Day 1:

. . . . . . . . . . . . . . . . .

## Our Light

## AFFIRMATION:

*"I am Light and free. I let go of anything that does not serve my purpose here. My purpose is joy, and _____ (fill in the blank only if you spontaneously feel moved)."*

One Hawaiian tradition speaks of the essence of a person as though we are a bowl of Light.[vi] Throughout our lives, our light gets dimmer if we allow our bowl to fill with rocks. It is our work to simply turn the bowl over, and let the stones fall out so that our light can shine resplendently again. I love that there is little effort required to shine brightly again since it is our nature—our birthright. Cleaning the clutter is all that is necessary.

In this step, our work is to identify what may be dimming our light and turn the bowl over. It may be as simple as clutter around you, emotionally or physically. If it doesn't bring you joy, let it go.

If any of the food in your pantry is depleting you rather than energizing you, let it go.

The dimming of my light sometimes occurs because of my busy calendar and the idea that I'm "overwhelmed" and "too busy" to do the things that I know are self-care related. Clearing my calendar of unnecessary appointments is like turning my bowl over to allow more light to shine.

The less we have to distract us, the clearer our essence becomes. It is our work to identify our distractions. It is better to be empty and free than completely filled with stuff that doesn't work for us. It can be wonderful to live with blank walls (no art or furnishings) until we find those pieces that really resonate with us. Remember you ARE free. Someone once said we are not here to find ourselves, rather, to create ourselves. Let it flow.

Journal about what you can drop from your calendar, your closet or your pantry. One less rock a day makes your life lighter, and your body will follow by naturally becoming lighter. This will be an ongoing project, but keep clearing something every day.

# Day 2:

. . . . . . . . . . . . . . . . . . . .

## Stillness

## AFFIRMATION:

*"I am not my thoughts. Like a hollow reed, I easily get out of my own way to feel Divine wisdom move through me."*

How do I stop and be still? How and why should I meditate? It is so foreign in Western Culture to appear to be doing nothing. If you already know the answers to these questions, please skip the rest of this explanation and move right into your meditation practice for at least 20 minutes.

It is not enough to clear the clutter from our environment outside of us, it is much more important to remove the clutter from our internal world, particularly the mind. Thinking is a tool for us to use in service for our spiritual purpose. More often, thought begins to run the show, and we forget how to turn it off. We worry. We fret. We talk incessantly. We analyze. We judge. We tell stories in our heads. It's like being in a conversation with someone who will not shut up, and we don't know how to walk away. Since our true essence is not all this chatter, all of this small talk just gets in the way of remembering who we really are! If we could turn off this chatter for a moment, or at least not identify with it, we might connect with our most profound wisdom and experience our essential Self.

When I find my emptiness and remember my Self, a soft smile usually comes over me, and I feel a deep love. I didn't DO anything to attain this state of contentment; I just stopped paying any attention to my thoughts, leaving me in an empty presence. From this nothingness, ANYTHING can emerge, well-being, wisdom, healing, and peace, regardless of my circumstance. This is like getting my "monkey mind" out of the way so I can listen to the Divine.

Once I experienced this space and the love that bubbles up naturally when I clear my mental chatter, I realized that I didn't need anything or anyone else to fill me up. I had access to the Divine inside me the entire time and therefore unlimited abundance of spiritual treasure—the kind we can actually take with us when we graduate from this world.

Find a quiet place to sit comfortably. Close your eyes and "drop-in" to your heart—that means bringing your attention to the center of your body. Take three deep breaths and then listen to your breath to draw your attention to something quiet and neutral. It gives your mind something to do that is less distracting. Let the thoughts float by paying no attention to them. Begin to feel the emptiness.

If this is new to you, practice this for at least 5 minutes a day. If your intention is simply to BE empty and BE curious about what might naturally bubble up from the depths of your soul, you may be pleasantly surprised. This is like turning your bowl over and letting the rocks drop out so you can feel your light again. Your attachment to and identification with your rational thoughts are the rocks.

Are you, like most of us, resisting this exercise? If this practice is so productive, then why do we resist it so much? Do any of these reasons apply to you:

- ♥ **FEAR OF THE UNKNOWN.** Western culture has taught me to value adventure OUTSIDE of myself but has never taught me to appreciate INNER self-exploration. It sounds dark and mysterious. What if there's a part of me that I don't want to see?

- ♥ **INSUFFICIENT TIME** to meditate, which is what I mostly tell myself. That's a convenient story. It's funny how I seem to find enough time for all the other important aspects of my life. The truth is that I don't value going inward as essential, and the story about time is just an excuse.

- ♥ **SURVIVAL.** If I become more interested in a quality spiritual experience and less interested in mere biological survival, my ego says, "I might not survive." The conversation in my head usually goes like this, "I have to go to work to pay the rent, so I'm not homeless, and pay the bills so I have electricity, and pay for groceries so I don't starve. That's why I can't take time to meditate."

- ♥ **FEAR OF CHANGE.** "What if my consciousness radically shifts and then my whole world shifts?" What if I discover that the world I spent my whole life building was an illusion, and not what I really came here to do. For example, I may have spent 30 years climbing the corporate ladder just to discover that when I reached the top, I had been climbing a ladder which was someone else's dream.

- ♥ **FEAR OF RESPONSIBILITY** for following the Divine's lead if I actually listened to it and knew my role in the cosmos. Knowing what needs to be done is not always easy, so I avoid listening to the Divine will.

- ♥ **FEAR OF FEELINGS.** If I stopped in silence, I would become aware of all the feelings I've been avoiding for so many years. That's too hard.

Do any of these excuses get in your way? Journal about what stops you from meditating. Meditate for at least 5 minutes a day anyway as a powerful practice and habit to explore your inner world.

# Day 3:

## The Source: Water

## AFFIRMATION:

*"I am so grateful for water. Water is my ally. Water effortlessly clears away all that is not Me."*

This is a process of Self-discovery and water can help us tremendously.

## WATER IS MEDICINE.

I heard about a doctor in prison in India that couldn't afford medications, so he prescribed drinking more water to his inmate patients, and it "cured them." If our bodies need to release toxins but don't have enough water to do so, the toxic waste will continue to stay in our bloodstream poisoning our cells and organs. It's time to wash away all toxins. Water can cure much suffering on many levels.

**Your body is mostly water.** You will find yourself bathing inside and out once you stop to appreciate the gift of water. Water conducts all of our electrical and chemical processes. Most of us fail to drink enough and end up dehydrated. An easy test is to grab a section of skin, pull it away from your bone and see if bounces back quickly or it takes time to return to its shape. If it takes time, then you are dehydrated. If you don't already do so, it is time to *carry a water bottle* with you at all times and surrender to the need to urinate more often.

**Quality matters.** We don't always treat ourselves to the purest water. Be sure your water doesn't contain poisonous chemicals like chlorine, chloramine (chlorine with ammonia) or fluoride. Find out where your water comes from and how it is treated. We often bottle it in plastic, which is poisonous to humans and the environment. Avoid plastic bottles that aren't BPA free!

**pH balance matters.** The earth is mostly water, and like us, it needs a specific pH, which is a measure of acidity to alkalinity. Think of your body like a saltwater aquarium that requires regular cleaning and balancing for pH. If an aquarium is too acid, the fish won't be able to see because their eyes will be etched and the acidity will eat away their fins. I actually saw this happen once and it is now happening to our oceans. The western diet is too acid, and we often don't often think about it. I've heard that cancer can only grow in a somewhat acidic environment. Like aquariums and the ocean, our bodies function best when the body's pH remains in balance. We can aid our body in controlling pH by not overeating acidic or alkaline foods.

**Purification.** As empaths, we have to learn how to protect ourselves from the toxic energy of others without building a wall around us by using food to pack on the pounds. One way to remove this negative energy is with water. I know a massage therapist who takes a salt bath every night before bed to wash off any energy she may have picked up from her clients that day. Another empathic friend has created a boundary by honoring her mantra, "people are in my life by invitation only." Thalassotherapy or taking a bath in salt washes away all that is unneeded, especially energy that doesn't belong to you. Taking a shower or going to the ocean is like a waterfall, full of negative ions that make us happy. Tears are healthy too. All of these practices are cleansing, honoring of our well-being and a gift us. Consider what kind of purification process works best for you and remember to do it when needed.

**Water is mystical.** Science is showing that water molecules have some kind of energetic memory.[vii] Water has been here for millions of years. It has "seen it all" from the air to the bottom of the deep sea, and has been part of millions of different bodies, plants, and animals. It carries all that memory, and those same ancient molecules have now formed 70% you're your current body. Because it is now part of you, you have mystical access to its energetic memory. In that sense, water assists us in remembering unity consciousness. Meditate on the nature of water and listen deeply to whatever wisdom it offers you.

**Spiritual Bathing.** Many faiths for millennia have used water for spiritual cleansing. You may be familiar with baptism in the Christian tradition, Mikvah in the Jewish tradition, or ablution before prayer in Islam. There are sacred springs around the world known for their healing properties. When not in Lourdes, you can create your own ritual bath just by setting sacred space and an intention. One of my favorite books on this subject is called "Spiritual Bathing: Healing Rituals and Traditions from Around the World[viii]."

Give yourself a sacred bath, drink lots of water and journal about its wisdom.

# Day 4:

## Devotion—An Antidote for Spiritual Amnesia

## AFFIRMATION:

*"I may be experiencing addiction, but I am not my addiction. I am so much bigger than that. I connect to my source, my soul, my core and remember myself as a Divine child. I choose to see each experience in this lifetime as a teacher of spiritual insight—an opportunity for spiritual growth—life lessons from which I expand to be more and more authentic and real."*

Deep down, we are here for connection. As social beings, we think it's about the connection with others, but as awakened spiritual beings, it is a first connection with the Divine—the Source. When we discover our relationship with the Source (refer to it as you wish, God, Goddess, Higher Power, etc.), it's like a love affair from which mystics write poetry, and David wrote the Psalms. This relationship is an endless supply of love, forgiveness, compassion, kindness, generosity and every other virtue we can imagine.

Since we are an aspect of the Divine, we must come to know our Higher Power not intellectually, but from within a relationship. Only by spending time together are relationships nurtured. That doesn't mean we should sit under a Bodhi Tree all day and meditate. That is not the way of the Feminine. Only by listening to the Divine will can we know our next call to action. This can occur all day long when we are working, cleaning, eating or brushing our teeth.

When it comes time to eat something, listen to your inner knowing—what does your body need right now to be healthy and vibrant? What food will energetically support your entire being?

If you feel drawn to food that you intellectually believe is "bad" for you, instead of judging that impulse, listen for its wisdom. Assume for a moment that a specific reason is drawing your entire being to that particular food. In your body's wisdom, perhaps you want food to feed an emotional need. Maybe you seek more sweetness in your life. Think of food as a metaphor for what you really want and be grateful for the lesson it offers.

If we stand in our devotion to our spiritual quest, we can apply spiritual wisdom to every feeling we generate, every decision we make and every action we take all day long. One of my most significant challenges has been to realize that my mundane activities ARE spiritual acts when I choose them in devotion. For example, my wisdom may remind me that eating chocolate cake all day may bring me short-lived joy, but not contribute to my long-term joy. Devotion to my commitment to a healthy and vibrant body gets me through those tempting moments. Through dedication to long-term joy, I can feel healthy in my body and be able to contribute to others.

Devotion to spiritual practices that work for me is necessary to remember my Self. For example, I like to practice ecstatic dance. I turn on my favorite uplifting music and dance spontaneously by myself to feel the joy of my heart express itself by moving my body. I do this physically to remember my joy and gratitude for being alive each day. The support I needed for this activity was a private space in which to dance, so my spouse built me a Lotus Belle tent in the backyard that doubles as a quiet meditation space.

Choose what spiritual practices work best for you, remind yourself WHY you do them, and then create a structure that supports your devotion.

# Day 5:

My Beautiful Body

## AFFIRMATION:

*"I am that I am, beautiful and radiant." (Say this affirmation while looking into your own eyes in the mirror).*

Do you shy away from mirrors? Mirrors are one of the most powerful tools we can use, physically and metaphorically, to reveal the truth about ourselves.

Our minds and stories about our bodies are so active that even a mirror won't help us sometimes. Some of us see a "fat person" in the mirror regardless of our anorexic state. What is your current conversation with yourself when you look in the mirror?

Try saying something like, "Wow I'm gorgeous! What a beautiful person inside and out! I am truly an extraordinary specimen of radiance, not to mention my fabulous features. What a strong and healthy body I have! I love my body soooooo much!"

If you find yourself resisting these kinds of statements, and your mind is saying, "but that's not true, I can't say that" then remember that whatever story you are telling yourself already isn't true either. We create our perception of reality with the stories we make up about it. The good news is that you can fake it until you make it!

Surrender to how you look in the mirror NOW. *Appreciate what's working and don't pay any attention to what isn't working for you.* This is actually a great approach to life in general, but let's starts with our fantastic, amazing, incredible bodies.

Now that you've given up harsh judgment about your OWN body try giving it up for others. We women seem to compare ourselves to other women, and it takes a victory of the human spirit to overcome this wiring. Many of us find ourselves judging the size of someone else's body and thinking, "well at least my thighs are smaller than hers." Make a list of the women in your life and write what you notice about THEIR bodies. Now that you are aware that you probably compare yourself to other women unconsciously *choose to give up the beauty competition.* Beauty pageants hurt women because they promote this competition, causing us to hate each other's beauty rather than celebrate everyone's unique qualities.

Eighty percent of women in the U.S. are dissatisfied with their appearance. And more than ten million are suffering from eating disorders.[ix] Begin to look for one thing that you find beautiful about yourself and compliment every woman you meet today. She's probably struggling with the same body image issues as everyone else.

# Day 6:

. . . . . . . . . . . . . . . . . .

## Coming Out of Hiding

## AFFIRMATION:

*"I have the courage to shine brightly whenever I choose. I choose to be fully Self-expressed in my beauty, my power, my freedom, and my authenticity."*

Now that we have celebrated each other's unique beauty, we may be feeling some resistance. There's a reason many women hide their beauty. Some of these feelings are often related to the following self-talk questions: What if I attract unwanted sexual attention? What if other women hate me because I'm beautiful? What if, because I care about my appearance, people judge me as vain or petty? What if it's scary to express my authentic beauty fully? What if the pretty girls were mean to me growing up and I don't want to be like them? These were all the questions I asked myself most of my life, and they stopped me from shining brightly.

When we realize that our real beauty radiates from the inside out, we have a choice to make—we can hide, or we can be Self-expressed. Flowers bloom knowing that they are the most vulnerable they have ever been, but it is for this glorious blooming that they come into existence at all.

We all have good reason to hide. I lived in Istanbul for a year when I was nineteen years old, and daily sexual assaults from strangers on the street were the norm. Women were taught to ignore this activity, and by the end, I was begging to hide in a full body covering as so many women do in some Islamic countries. It's no coincidence that I gained thirty pounds that year.

But there comes a time when we must take a stand. Tahirih, the great female poet from nineteenth Century Iran, removed her veil in public saying, "You may kill me as soon as you like, but you will never stop the emancipation of women." She was put to death for this act but was never forgotten. I share this because hiding our beauty has been a way to create safety and survival for thousands of years.

It is a new age, an age of female power in which we emerge and stand firm in the face of danger. The feminine is necessary to balance the masculine if humanity is going to survive. A heroine of this new age is Malala, a little girl in Afghanistan under Taliban rule who risked her life to go to school every day. She is a survived a shot to the head and continues to stand for the education of girls to this day.[x]

These women are my heroines because they remind me of the courage that we all have inside us. The courage to be authentic is a daily test for me. I pray for the courage to stand in my beauty, in my feminine power, to be both strong and vulnerable and to be authentic on a daily basis. I know that as I push the envelope, it makes the path to freedom easier for others.

Although we still have rampant violence against women, at least now we don't think it is acceptable behavior. We HAVE come a long way! We no longer remove our ribs to have smaller waists. We no longer bind our feet to make them more petite. We no longer use urine of young boys to 'treat' our freckles. We no longer have hysterectomies to treat our "hysteria." Lobotomies are no longer used to control our behavior. We are no longer burned at the stake (except in rural areas of India).

These are REAL fears that run through our blood, and they are why it takes courage for us to come out of hiding. In this age of feminine power, when we DO choose to show up, our innate beauty shines in our facial expressions, our body language, our clothing, our homes, our career and relationship choices.

Now, let me share something vulnerable. I have chosen to express myself playfully as a mermaid. As a mermaid, I embody freedom, sovereignty, profound wisdom, beauty, power, and carefree delight.[3] It may seem ironic that I feel more authentic as a mermaid than I ever did as a lawyer of twenty years. As a lawyer, I was trained to be a gentleman, wear a suit, lower the pitch of my voice, detach from my emotions, pretend that I knew more than others about their problems and get paid to fix those issues. I admit I didn't have to go that route. It is theoretically possible to be a feminine lawyer.

---

[3] You can friend me on Facebook as Vyana Reynolds (my mermaid name). I founded Kona Mermaid School and run Mermaid Dreams Bed & Breakfast in Kona, Hawaii.

It's hard to believe in something I've never seen before. Funny, that's what most people say about mermaids.

I hope my embodiment pushes the envelope for you. If I can be a mermaid, then you can be ANYTHING. Perhaps you haven't met or explored a mythic part of yourself yet.

# Day 7:

· · · · · · · · · · · · · · · · · ·

## Intuition

## AFFIRMATION:

*"I trust my inner knowing[4] and am healed on all levels: physical, emotional, and spiritual. I am grateful for my body and how it creates symptoms to remind me of the deeper healing opportunities."*

One of humanity's superpowers is its ability to connect with our inner knowing—our intuition. This kind of knowing is different from the intellectual knowledge found in the memory cells of the brain. This type of knowing feels like a "gut" instinct. This is a feeling navigation that provides insight into the nature of things that is not obvious from the outside.

Intuition can access the subconscious, which is the driving force behind addictive behavior. If addictive reality were conscious, we would just use willpower to stop being addicts. Every addict knows that willpower is not enough!

---

[4] *While I am intellectually aware that knowingness is the noun form of knowing, I choose to use 'knowing' as both a verb and noun because it sounds better to me.*

One woman I know "muscle tests" all her food before she puts it in her mouth. That means she uses her body's inner knowing to tell her if the food will support her health or deplete her. For example, she holds the food in a relaxed way and asks the question, "Will eating this apple nourish my body?" If her body leans forward, the answer is yes. If her body seems to lean backward, the answer is no. She tries to stay mentally neutral so her body can tell the truth without interference.

Learning to ask this question, even of our conscious mind, would be a great idea, but many of us have begun not to trust our addicted minds. As we listen more to our intuition, we will become wiser at knowing when our conscious mind is deceiving us. For example, sometimes my mind will say, "Oh what the heck, what's one more potato chip in the grand scheme of things." My intuition doesn't even have to think about it, it just knows that potato chips don't serve me.

People are beginning to see intuition as a gift and honing it more and more, not just to heal themselves, but also to become medical intuitives. We've started to understand that the symptoms we experience in our bodies are usually a manifestation of an emotional or spiritual upset that needs healing. That's why ancient techniques of energetic healing are coming back into style (Reiki, homeopathy, acupuncture, craniosacral, aquatic bodywork). Now, instead of resisting my food cravings by resenting them, I can be grateful that they are pointing me to something much deeper need that wants my attention.

That's why I love Louise Hays' book, *You Can Heal Your Life.*[xi] She uses her intuition to identify the underlying emotional cause of a physical symptom. I'm not saying that her diagnosis is accurate for everyone, but it's a great starting point to ask our intuition what is really going on in our emotional or energetic body that would create a particular symptom. For example, my chronic yeast infections began after my first intercourse experience at age 22 outside of marriage. Although it was a positive encounter, it triggered the same sexual shame that followed "playing doctor" as a child with my friends. I was raised to believe that sexual activity outside of marriage was "bad," so I harshly judged myself and was afraid of being found out. I now release any shame and own my sexuality as part of being a healthy human being. I now believe that childhood curiosity is healthy, and my shame was just a story. Unconscious suffering is not a powerful way to live. Listening more deeply to our intuition is the key to a better life and exploring our subconscious can be of enormous benefit.

I've successfully approached my subconscious in several ways: by remembering my dreams, through hypnosis, archetypal embodiment, meditation, with spontaneous writing or art, and by connecting with human intuition (my own and others).

Questions are a great way to let answers flow from the subconscious. The magic lies in giving birth to "the question." Start with simple questions. "What am I most afraid others will find out about me?" "Right now, what would the Divine want me to know to support my healing?" "How could I be freer?" "Where am I feeling stuck?" "Why am I in certain relationships?" "Where am I feeling pain?" "Have I felt this pain before in my life?" "Am I happy?" "What's my burden?" "What dream have I not fulfilled?" "What matters most to me?"

Once our intuition leads us to the core of the matter, often in layers, like peeling an onion, we will be able to consciously address our wounds, forgive and heal. Magically, healing is also possible without conscious understanding, we can just ask for healing on all levels regardless. Have you asked lately?

# BONUS TOOLS FOR STEP 3

1. Fill a backpack with some heavy rocks.

    Take it for a walk on the beach when there are few people around, especially swimmers. At the beach, take out a rock and give it a name like "my incomplete past relationship," or like "my attachment to drinking Coca-Cola," or like "my abandonment fears" or like whatever weighs you down. Declare yourself free of that issue and throw the rock as far as you can into the ocean. Let the universe do the rest.

2. Be "in empty presence"

    ...(see exercise from Day 2 of Step 3) with your support team during your weekly meeting and share from there.

3. Stop unconsciously using small talk

    ...with others to avoid emotional intimacy; it wastes our life energy. I like to use food this way at a party. If my mouth is busy, then I don't have to talk to people, or worse, to listen to them. If you want to feel connected to others and have meaningful relationships, take the conversation deeper by asking things like, "What's real for you right now?"; "What are your passions in life?"; "What would you be doing if you didn't have to work and money was no issue?" As you begin to share what's real for you in a more way, you will find that others will follow your lead. We are all hungry for more emotional intimacy, but often afraid to go there.

## 4. Try Colon hydrotherapy.

When my pH is out of balance, most of my sugar cravings come from a yeast infection that lives in my colon. After a colonic, my sugar cravings magically disappear. Health begins in the colon! Colon health is also critical for our immune system. I need a healthy immune system to have a healthy thyroid. I need my thyroid to balance my weight and hunger.

## 5. Have a mythic dinner party.

If you want to meet a part of yourself that you've never met before, throw a mythic dinner party. Everyone must come as his or her mythic-Self and be in character all evening! You may discover that some of your friends are really angels, fairies, unicorns, kings, queens, bards, friendly dragons or even elves. Be sure to tell them to bring a healthy food dish to share. You are creating a magical realm where anything is possible—even healthy food that also tastes delicious.

# STEP 4:

·················

*Create a Life You Love*

# Day 1:

## Create Your Own Reality

### AFFIRMATION:

*"I powerfully create my reality and my experiences by the stories I tell myself and others. I am a master storyteller."*

I heard a story once about two identical twin boys where each received a shovel and told to clean up a horse's stall full of manure. One boy hated life because cleaning manure was a stinky dirty job. The other boy was excited to accomplish the same task because he thought, "There must be a pony in here somewhere!" The entire universe conspires to provide the pony when it hears this desire. Wouldn't YOU want to give a pony to this grateful little boy? That's why crowdfunding has been so successful. We all want to conspire to manifest our dreams together.

We make things mean something because we humans are wired to want more than mere survival. That is how we experience fulfillment or disappointment. Depending on the meaning we assign to our experience, we create our own perception of reality. Then we forget it was just a story we made up, and we think IT IS REAL. Our emotional reaction to the story now makes us FEEL IT IS REAL. Have you ever said, "You hurt my feelings?" Wouldn't it be freeing to know that no one has the power to hurt your feelings ever again?

*Our power is in remembering the difference between what really happened and the story we made up about it.* The story is an illusion—it's not what actually happened. We create our reality this way every day and call it our past. Our past then becomes our future ONLY because we recreate the same story repeatedly with different players and circumstances. Does this sound familiar?

If like most humans, you are resisting this concept, it is only because you want to be "right." We all want to be right. The only problem with being right all the time is the price we pay—pain, suffering, isolation, loss of connection, war, sadness, anger, powerlessness, and the list goes on. If you are willing to give up being "right" and more interested in creating *a story that works for YOU,* you will be free to create whatever you desire in your future *regardless of the circumstances.*

You can identify stories that aren't working for you by asking yourself what makes you feel resigned and cynical, powerless or judgmental. Use your journal to rewrite at least one disempowering story you tell yourself. At first, it will pretend to be REAL and refuse to be called just a "story." That's normal. Just keep writing. After you've told the same victim story over and over again, it gets boring (for everyone), so you'll notice that you don't want to tell it anymore.

Ask yourself, "How is that story working for me? Does it make me happy, feel loved and create more love for others?" If your answer is no, then make up a new story. Once you surrender your attachment to the old story, you can easily make up a new one that works better for the future you desire to create, since we just make everything up anyway. If there is a TRUTH out there about what happened, only our Higher Power can see all perspectives on it. Understanding that our vision can be limited in its perception helps us give up the idea that we have to be "right" all the time.

If you are stuck, it may be because some things that happen ARE real. Suppose my friend said, "You look fat in those pants." The fact that she said those words is REAL, but the story I make up about it later, like, "she's a jerk" is not. Thinking that she said these words on purpose to make me feel bad" is NOT real. It's just a disempowering story about what happened. An alternative story might be, "My friend may be struggling with her own weight and afraid that other women are competing with her. I'll check out my story by asking her to have coffee with me, and I'll offer her compassion, a listening ear, and assure her that we are not in competition. This is a great opportunity for connection."

You may have noticed that the second story was not about "me." You may have noticed that it is often humanity's first response—to take everything personally and make it about ME. Why? Because humans often fear that, we are "not enough," and that we are the center of the universe. Now that you know this about humans, you can laugh about it. Without judgment, *we are now free* to make a different choice.

Distinguishing what actually happened from the story that I made up about it is the key and is not an easy task when emotions run high. What's worse is when our friends and families agree with our stories and make them even more real, thinking loyalty in storytelling is a kindness. It's actually a conspiracy, and when done in significant numbers can cause much suffering.

Now is the time to dismantle what no longer serves you, so that you have a blank canvas on which to write your new story. Begin in your journal.

# Day 2:

. . . . . . . . . . . . . . . . .

## Declare your future

## AFFIRMATION:

*[You will generate your own affirmation today—see below].*

If you're sitting in your car and looking out the windshield, you're looking mostly into your future, where you are headed. If you look in the rearview mirror, you can see the past. This mirror is tiny in proportion to the windshield. That's because you would never arrive at your desired destination if all you did were to look in the rearview mirror.

The present experience mostly consists of the stories of the past and reflects decisions made in the past. If I were to focus on the present moment, I might say, "Hi, I'm Heather, and I'm a food addict." This is how the traditional 12 Step Program works. Instead, I find it more useful to declare the future I want to live into, "Hi, I'm Heather, and I'm freedom, carefree delight, and abundance." When generating your future, be careful that the words you choose are not a reaction against the past, but are independently inspiring. As you say the words, be sure to generate the feeling they stand for. Actually, feel the freedom, delight, and abundance when you speak them, for example.

Be careful to avoid negatives. When Nixon said, "I'm not a crook," all we heard was the word "crook." That's how the universe works too. It is not as empowering to say "I am not a food addict" as it is to say, "I am powerful and free to eat healthy food as I choose." (See the list of possibilities you may wish to generate in Exhibit A to get you started.) Add your own! Keep it short and straightforward, so you can easily remember it. Whatever possibility you generate is your affirmation today!

Your words are more powerful than you realize. Ancient languages such as Hebrew and Hawaiian knew that each sound had its own vibrational frequency. Our bodies and the material world consist of a bunch of atoms, electrons, and neutrons. They were attracted to each other and decided to stick together as molecules because they seemed to like each other's vibration. This is an excellent example of how science and "magical thinking" are actually one and the same. Science is what we call things we have figured out how to measure, and magic is science that we don't understand yet. Therefore, when the breath of life passes your lips with focused intention, it sets the entire universe in motion. That's one reason prayer has been known to work! What if you suddenly declared that time should stand still, for example. You might be surprised to find that the entire universe wants to play along just for the fun of it. That's the kind of power you wield in your word.

When people ask how you are, instead of saying, "Fine," use words to create the future you desire, such as, "I'm getting healthier and happier every day!" Circle words you like on Exhibit A and use them more and more in your speaking. Write them on "post-its" all over the house.

Listen to music lyrics that uplift and inspire you such as, "I Can See Clearly Now, the Rain is Gone.[xii]" You might want to write yourself a theme song to live into and sing it in the shower or car every day. Exhibit B contains my theme song.

Write a Declaration of the future (called a Sacred Trust) that you are creating for yourself and the world. Think big, even beyond your lifetime, of the difference your presence and your dreams can make on this planet. Martin Luther King's dream for racial equality has lasted far beyond his physical life. See Exhibit C for my Sacred Trust.

# Day 3:

· · · · · · · · · · · · · · · · · ·

## Vision Your Future

## AFFIRMATION:

*"When I envision my future and take the first step, the universe responds with enthusiasm to make all my dreams come true."*

I've heard that many professional athletes spend a lot of time envisioning themselves being successful. Why—because it works! They see themselves performing flawlessly in their mind's eye, and it's as good if not better than a physical practice.

In practice, sometimes we miss the shot and lose faith in ourselves. When we see ourselves making the shot repeatedly in our brain, however, it builds our confidence, and the body doesn't seem to know the difference.

Visioning is one of our greatest allies. Pictures speak thousands of words. Now create a vision board[5] that you can see each day to

---

[5] *A vision board is a collection of images that inspire you to create a life you love. You may want to cut pictures out of a magazine and glue them on a poster board, for example. It is easily accessible so you can see it at least once a day and be reminded of the future you are creating.*

remind you of the future you are living. Let yourself really enjoy the feeling of the fulfillment, as if it has already happened. Your job is just to vision it and say "thank you." Let the universe take care of the "how." By "how" I mean how it will be achieved.

A wise woman shared a metaphor with me. She said, "When you use your Global Positioning System (GPS) to get to your destination in your car, you don't argue with it about the route. The GPS considers traffic patterns and determines the shortest route. Your job is to start the car, turn on the GPS, and follow the path that was set before you. It may not be the path YOU would have chosen, but it usually works out better than if you had planned it yourself." It is our job to tell the universe where we want to go. Take the first step, and do not worry about "how" we are going to get there, except to have an open mind that it may look different from what we would have anticipated. In her case, the route included a bankruptcy, which freed her to say "yes" to her dream when it came looking for her. Her dream knew to find her because it was all over her vision board!

Surround yourself with people, books, activities, movies, and music that support your vision. Release any distractions.

Identify people or aspects of the Divine that you admire. Who are your heroes? Invite them to be on your "board of directors" for your life. You can go to them with your etheric body for wise counsel when you find yourself at a crossroad. Let their lives inspire you to expand even further. My board includes my fairy godmother (Ariel Spilsbury), Mahatma Gandhi, Malala Yousafzai, Oprah Winfrey, Lady Godiva, Quan Yin, and Gilda Radner, the comedian.

Visioning is so powerful that, like affirmations, it will serve you to take a few moments every day, perhaps before bed, to look at your vision board and let yourself enjoy the feeling of it as if it has already manifested in your life.

# Day 4:

............

## Metaphors to Live By

## AFFIRMATION:

*"I focus my attention on the beauty all around me and 'what is working' in my life. I trust the rest will resolve itself."*

Maybe it's just me, but in this busy world, I often forget all this spiritual wisdom. I need an easy way to remember, especially when I get in the middle of an emotional crisis. Metaphor, parables and memory tools can help.

For example in the 12 Step Program, I learned the acronym, "HALT." It stands for **H**ungry, **A**ngry, **L**onely, or **T**ired, to remind me that when I'm in one of these four states, I am most likely to fall back into addictive behavior. If I find myself in one of these four states, it is time to call my buddy and get the support and self-care that I need.

To overcome addictive behavior or compulsive eating, we must cultivate wisdom! That is one of the gifts of any suffering. Here is an example of a story that reminds me to be open-minded and to receive the wisdom I seek:

# A CUP OF TEA

*A Japanese master received a university professorwho came to inquire about Zen.*

*The master served tea. He poured his visitor's cup full,and then kept on pouring.*

*The professor watched the overflow until he no longer could restrain himself.*

*"It is overfull. No more will go in!"*

*"Like this cup," the master said, "you are full of your own opinions and speculations. How can I show you Zen unless you first empty your cup?"[xiii]*

Begin to identify the wisdom you have already gathered in this lifetime and write it down in a separate journal, so you don't have to learn those same lessons again and again. Since you won't read that book every day, try to find a metaphor, song, poem or parable for each piece of wisdom to help remind you of it when you really need it.

Christ was a pro at parables. He regularly used metaphor so his followers could do 3 things:

1. Be open to listening (everyone likes stories).

2. Interpret it in any way they wanted (freedom of thought).

3. Remember the wisdom of his teachings.

The metaphor also makes the listener work for the meaning, like solving a mystery. Working for something makes us value it more. This approach works well with my three-year-old inner child who wants to run the show and eat candy all day. One of my favorite parables is about the carcass of a dead dog in a narrow alley. Jesus and his disciples passed by, and the stench was terrible. It had been dead for some time. The disciples lifted their robes to avoid it. Jesus knelt down and looked carefully at the carcass saying, "What beautiful white teeth it has."[6]

This story reminds me to focus on what is beautiful and what is working in my life, rather than focusing on the "problem." If I pay attention and appreciate what I want more of, it will increase. If I focus on what I don't like, it too will grow.

That's why I never count calories or get on a scale much anymore! I will know whether I am healthy from the way I feel or how my clothes fit. By focusing on my healthy self-care, the extra weight will take care of itself. For self-care, I focus on getting moving in fun ways, getting enough rest, connecting with those I love, eating delicious, high-quality food, and of course, spiritual nourishment.

When I look in the mirror at my body, I look for only what it is

---

[6] *Many tales about the life of Christ circulated and never made it to the canonical Gospels but continued to be told by both Christians and Muslims. This story appears in a number of important Muslim sources, such as the Musibat-nama of Farid al-Din Attar (a 13th century poet and mystic).*

beautiful and focus on that alone! What are your favorite features? Do you love your hair, your soft skin or your eyes most? Revel in what you love about yourself and others. Let them know! Journal about it.

# Day 5:

Being vs. Doing

## AFFIRMATION:

*"I am free NOW. I always was free and always will be. I am exactly where I need to be. There is nothing to fix. All is well."*

While I encourage each of us to be "in action," when we are moved authentically, it is simply more important to BE. No action is actually required to be free. Freedom is a state of being. That means you could choose to be free RIGHT NOW—actually, we always were free; we just forgot! From this state of BEing, actions will naturally follow in alignment. That's how problems take care of themselves even though we take our attention off them. Let's try it...

***Generate the feeling of well-being*** that comes from total acceptance of yourself just as you are and just as you are not with all of your "imperfections, " including any tendency toward compulsive eating or addictive habits. How does it feel to stop making yourself "wrong"? How does it feel to love yourself regardless? YOU generate that feeling – it comes from telling yourself a different story. There's nothing wrong here! There's nothing to fix! Begin to notice when you don't feel "good," and what story you are telling yourself. Choose a different story that feels better.

For example, most of my life, I retold the story that "something was wrong." I would find evidence for that everywhere because then I could be right about it. I could tell you what was wrong with my body—hips are too big—my pants don't fit, and with politics—corruption and irresponsibility. I would find that in my relationships, people's drama depleted me, and in my closet, I would find that I didn't have enough clothes. In my bank account, there was never enough money. I would find evidence everywhere in my life that "something was wrong." When I realized that I was actually creating the story that "something is wrong," I decided to choose a new one: "The entire universe is conspiring to surprise and delight me." Now I find evidence for that reality—and it's way more fun! *I've become a magic moment collector.*

It doesn't matter if your story is "true" because we are limited in our personal perception of reality anyway. Change the pattern and "voila"—new reality. New reality automatically creates new feelings.

This means you are not just free from food addiction at this moment (because you choose that), but you are free to make a different experience out of ANY circumstance in your life. There is no circumstance where you are not free. Imagine that you could be imprisoned for life because of circumstances and still be "free" because you decide to.

On the inner plane, you can choose to create whatever story or experience you desire. The Italian movie, "Life is Beautiful," is one of the greatest examples of how you can create your own story. In the movie, a father turned the concentration camp experience during the Holocaust into a "game" of winning a tank for his young son. He kept a sense of humor and modeled how life could be beautiful even under those circumstances. The son believed that the entire experience was just a game and he actually "won" a ride on the tank in the end. If being a prisoner during the Holocaust can become a game you can "win," then the circumstances of our lives do not have to control us, and we are always free.

In my case, I choose to believe that I am really a mermaid, born to a human family with a disability—legs. I was over 40 years old when I finally acquired a prosthetic tail to help me swim like myself again. Although being a mermaid doesn't wholly define me, since I'm so much more, it does give me more freedom. Mermaids don't live in a box. They're sovereign, free and powerful, not to mention magical. By choosing to live a mythic life, I have an excuse to play big. When I dress in the morning, I don't have to worry about over-doing it. I'm free to dye my hair any color I want.

When I meet someone who seems stuck in a job he or she hates, I ask him or her what their dream is. They tell me, and I sprinkle magical glitter into their world and tell them that their dreams will come true. They always do anyway—but when blessed by a magical mermaid –an acceleration of the manifestation of their dreams may occur. I'm not acting in a costume. I'm BEING a mermaid.

If you were to live a mythic life, what would it look like? Would you be a Goddess, angel, fairy, coyote, king, divine fool, whale, Jaguar, dragon, shaman, empress, alien, queen, priestess, or just a bigger YOU? What inspires you? Try it on. You're not "doing" something as much as you are "being" something. YOU are much more significant than you remember. Meet the parts of yourself you may not have met yet. Give yourself the gift of freedom to BE as big as you really are! Here are three tips:

1. If you have to, fake it till you make it.

2. You don't have to tell anyone else at first.

3. When the rest of the world responds differently to you than ever before, your small Self wouldn't usually NOT know what to do. So, you must muster your Mythic Self to understand how to "be" at that moment.

For example, if while you were BEING a great writer, someone was inspired to fund your dream of being a writer and handed you a check for a significant amount, your small self might not feel worthy to receive it. It is critical that you continue BEING your mythic Self at that moment, and graciously receive the support the universe wants to provide you.

# Day 6:

## Abundance Thinking

## AFFIRMATION:

*"I CAN have it all. We can ALL have it ALL."*

When I first said to myself "I can have it all," it was 9:00 p.m. on a Monday night in August 2015. I didn't believe this statement at the time, but my coach had just asked me to try it on. I figured it didn't hurt to play along. I had been looking for a small vacation home in Hawai'i with the idea that someday I would retire there. I had two limiting beliefs: (1) I didn't have enough money to buy the house of my dreams and (2) it would take at least 20 years before I could afford to retire in Hawai'i.

In the mindset, "I can have it all," I went to the internet to search for the house of my dreams at an exact location and elevation. THERE IT WAS—the first house that popped on the screen. It was a beautifully landscaped cedar home on two acres of land in Kona,

Hawaii, at my preferred elevation, and only ten minutes away from the ocean. It had five bedrooms, five bathrooms, high ceilings and wood floors, and was way more money than I imagined I could afford for a "vacation" home.

Keep in mind that I spent the first 35 years of my life in debt, owing $135,000 in student loans when I graduated from law school. Just 6 years before finding my dream house, I had come out of a divorce that left me $10,000 in the red! I had lost all of my retirement savings and my home. I was able to keep my solo law practice and rent an apartment in the San Francisco Bay Area. I was not alone in my scarcity experience; as I had just made it through the great recession of 2008, where so many Americans lost everything.

The magic of the moment occurred when I read the very last sentence of the advertisement for my dream home. It read, *"This has been a bed & breakfast for over twenty five years and comes with a permit."* Running a bed and breakfast had never occurred to me before. It was 10:00 p.m. when I woke my husband and introduced him to the idea. He was thrilled and well suited to help manage a bed and breakfast in Hawaii. We immediately made an offer, and he flew to Hawaii to see it within fourth eight hours. They accepted our offer, and everything fell effortlessly into place. Why wait twenty years to "retire" in Hawaii, if we can go now? Although I would never have orchestrated running a bed and breakfast myself, I was open to HOW the universe was responding to my ultimate dream of creating a mermaid retreat and healing center.

If the universe is conspiring to make all our dreams come true, then the only thing that could possibly get in the way is our own limiting beliefs. Where did these limiting beliefs come from? When we were children, we made up stories about how the world seemed to work. We collected evidence to support our stories, and they became beliefs. Those beliefs are often about time, money and worthiness. They seem so real, that we don't think of them as limiting beliefs, just as real. They become our blind spots. Here's an example.

Let's say you went to school for thirteen years (preschool through high school) where there weren't enough supplies for everyone or enough books, and the teacher wasn't paid enough. Your training would convince you to believe "there wasn't enough." You might spend the rest of your life unconsciously collecting evidence to support this experience. Is it any wonder why most of our country continues to struggle in this scarcity paradigm?

Let's say you were born, instead, into a family of wealth, where the only question you had to answer each morning was, "What shall I spend all this money on? I have more than I can possibly spend!" You know you can have anything you desire, and *you never settle for less.*

Ask yourself, if money were no issue, would you do things differently? Where are you settling for less? *Imagine that you've just won the lottery. Make a list of all the things you will do with the money.* YOU decide how much money you've won.[xiv]

STOP! Important: Don't continue reading until you have completed this exercise.

Great job! Most people start the exercise listing things like a beautiful home, a new car, a vacation, and the like. After meeting their personal desires, most people get bored with their material wealth and look for ways to contribute to others. After fulfilling YOUR dreams, the greatest joy becomes "making a difference" in the lives of others, because you know that the universe wants everyone's dreams to come true.

Now, the second part of the abundance exercise is to realize that *the list you just made after winning the lottery is a list of things you came here to be and do.* It is your work to take the first step and let the universe figure out the "how." It is time for your limited thinking about time and money to move aside and allow the universe to fill in the blanks for you. Tell yourself that you CAN have it all! It is time to play big.

You can apply the same exercise to time. What would you do if you had unlimited time? Do you say you're too old to go back to school? Would you start a new career if you had time? Would you travel the world? Make a list of dreams as though time were not a consideration. Add these dreams to your vision board.

# Day 7:

. . . . . . . . . . . . . . . .

## Cultivating Gratitude

## AFFIRMATION:

*"Thank you, thank you and thank you. I am so grateful for every facet of my life, of this planet and the opportunity to be here."*

The fastest way to manifest a life you love is to be grateful for everything you have been given! When we first arrived on this planet, we had nothing except our cute little baby bodies, but it took many years before we developed to be self-sufficient. In the meantime, someone must have changed our diapers and fed us. Why? Because, we're precious beings!

We are born with this generosity. Have you ever met an "entitled" teenager who thinks the world owes him or her something? In my experience, that attitude seems to dry up any trace of generosity quickly. The universe responds to us in the same way when we fail to be grateful for everything it provides.

The fastest way to prime the blessing pump is to express gratitude. That miracle is just the icing on the cake. The most profound blessing of living from a state of gratitude is how it changes our own perception of reality. By being in a state of gratitude, we see our lives differently. If I've already enjoyed more than a lifetime of blessings, then whatever is to come is just gravy—not something I'm expecting. Each day feels like my birthday, and all I have to do is open presents for the rest of my life.

## START A SPECIAL GRATITUDE JOURNAL.

Schedule a time every day to write down at least five things or people you are grateful for—be specific. Don't forget to include yourself in particular. Share at least one thing you are grateful for with at least one person every day. Begin to live in a state of gratitude for everything.

When we first start this practice, we write about the most obvious blessings such as our home, our food, our partners, friends, and other beneficial gifts. Once you have all those down, move to the next level of gratitude even in the face of things that appear on the surface to be adversarial.

Let's take my love/hate relationship with food for example. It's hard to create a healthy relationship with food if I blame it for creating my suffering. I could tell you about binging, self-hatred and total food misery, but that is just an old "victim" story. Aside from feeling like comrades in our food hell, I would not be serving either of us. Alternatively, I could tell you what I've learned from my approach to food as an adversary.

I've learned compassion for the suffering of others. I've learned to forgive myself. I've learned that I can create a life I love in spite of such challenges. I've learned to love and accept myself unconditionally. I've learned that real beauty expresses itself from the inside-out, not the other way around. I've learned to ask for help and to be grateful. In short, I have gleaned my greatest spiritual treasures from one of my greatest challenges.

Now that I've had that experience, I've decided that suffering is NOT the only way to collect spiritual insights. I could have learned them in a dream, for example, without needing to manifest the suffering in the third dimension. I could alternatively have learned these lessons from a state of bliss and ecstasy since wisdom is available everywhere.

For example, I recently moved to Hawaii to be able to swim with the dolphins in the wild. They have taught me to value play, rest, harmony, and simplicity. They are masters of joy! I've enjoyed this privilege for the time that I've been here. It appears that a new legislation may pass shortly; a law that could fine swimmers up to $100,000 if we are within fifty yards of a dolphin. In my personal experience, politics motivates the law, not the well-being of dolphins. I could be furious about this turn of events from the perspective of, "I have the right to be near dolphins in the wild as long as I am not harming them." My rights appear trampled using this perspective and injustice has occurred.

In contrast, I could feel grateful to have been able to connect with them for the time that we did have together. What a blessing! Using this frame of reference frees me to take political action to preserve respectful dolphin swimming from a clear mental state rather than from reactionary anger. Anger is not attached to this state of being; thus, any stand I decide to take does not generate as much resistance from others. From this viewpoint, I can even listen to my adversaries and better understand their position while being grateful for their perspective. This kind of listening can be very disarming. This state of being is FREE to make whatever choice feels appropriate at the time. I'm flexible to change my mind or offer a compromise. Self-righteous entrenchment in one position can create a lot of suffering for everyone.

Zealous fanaticism is born from self-righteous anger. Entrenched anger is toxic. Imagine how different the world would be if fanatics became grateful and generous toward others, while still holding true to their core values? The universe would respond to them in kind, and they would accomplish so much more. Mostly, fanatics just get a lot of pushback, not because their agenda occurs "crazy" to others, but because the energy behind their agenda feels dangerous to others. Gentle "crazy" doesn't threaten us; it's the combination of angry and "crazy" that we fear.

Let go of your anger and other negative emotions by replacing them with gratitude and generosity. Are you a food Nazi to yourself? Is there only one way to create a food and exercise plan? Where does it feel like you are beating your head against a wall? Where are you feeling self-righteous and not listened to? Apply gratitude and see what happens.

If all any of us got out of this program were gratitude, it would be more than enough.

# STEP 5:

......................

## *Sovereignty*

# Day 1:

. . . . . . . . . . . . . . . . .

## What is Sovereignty?

## AFFIRMATION:

*"I claim my sovereignty."*

The Divine Feminine takes many forms, and one resembles Artemis (a Greek Goddess) or Diana (the Roman Goddess), and she was more recently reinvented in the movies as Katniss Everdeen from the Hunger Games and as Wonder Woman. She is here to remind us of our sovereignty and our feminine "superpowers." She can appear to be a warrior.

Sovereignty means to act in alignment with our inner knowing rather than what the world thinks we "should" do.

I spent most of my life doing what I "should" do rather than what was right for me. I followed the rules and always walked on the side-walk to play safe. I sought security and power within a masculine paradigm. I thought that if I played the dominant game and applied discipline and intelligence, I could beat them at their own game. After all, the competition was the whole idea. After experiencing a lifetime of unfair treatment, human rights were the game I wanted to play, and I wanted to win for the benefit of women-kind. I even learned to draft and pass federal legislation in Washington, D.C. for this purpose.

After 24 years of traditional schooling, I went to battle each day as a lawyer fighting for civil rights. Even though I won my legal cases against racism, rape and sexual harassment, the systematic frame-work was flawed, and my clients were re-victimized by it. They may have won money, but they lost emotionally. After one year, I realized that within this adversarial paradigm, it really was almost impossible to "win" even if you "won" the case. Just like in the Hunger Games, even if the tribute won the game created by the Capitol, he/she would have become a murderer of other oppressed children in the process. I don't consider that a win. In the movie Wonder Woman, she won the war but validated the culture of war in the process.

Artemis, on the other hand, ran with her own tribe and created her own rules, symbiotic with nature. She relied on the natural world to sustain her. She did not rely on men and did not marry. Her com-panions were female, much like the Amazonian culture in which Wonder Woman was raised—except that there was no emphasis on war. I'm not suggesting a world without men. I'm suggesting a world that is not based on domination and one, which values the feminine aspects of our nature.

These epic stories give me three inspirations:

1.  Freedom to be authentically powerful.

2.  Courage to be sovereign.

3.  Wisdom to know what game I am playing, and who wrote the rules.

In the past, power was the basis of brute force. The tide is turning, and as humanity evolves, power is in truth-telling, creativity, and virtues. Malala[ix] is an excellent example of this. This little girl in Afghanistan spoke out against the Taliban regime that refused to allow girls to attend school. She did not buy into the power of their guns, and she continued courageously to speak out. They shot her from which she has recovered, more persistently than ever. Malala is now a voice for girls worldwide. She is a leader of truthntelling. When the Taliban regime has withered away, Malala will return to her country as a leader to reestablish a culture of peace and education for everyone. The question for each of us is, am I authentically self-expressed? Am I speaking my truth? Am I wearing what I choose, or is it something I "should" wear? Is my job working for me or am I just doing what I'm told?

The purpose of a support group in this process is to help us find the courage to answer these questions AND take a stand. If we don't find the courage to be and do what we came here for, our bodies will let us know that we are not in alignment with ourselves. Our bodies never lie. They tell us what we are too afraid to say. It can show up as physical symptoms. In my case, my underactive thyroid is improving the more I speak my truth. The throat area is associated with speech. It also helps if I sing and laugh. I thank my thyroid, for reminding me!

The third inspiration—***Wisdom to know what game we're playing***—makes me the most excited! This is where we get to find our blind spots. It's hard for a fish to know it's in water until it jumps out.

For example, if the children in the Hunger Games had made up their own rules and decided to cooperate with one another rather than follow the rules and kill each other, they would have undermined the purpose of the games. Discontinuation of the games would have resulted. We are all going to die at some point anyway, so whose rules will we choose to follow in the meantime?

At age twenty-six, I played the law school "game." In law school, the women's test scores were higher coming in, but men were getting the higher grades upon graduation (which mattered greatly for job selection). I wondered what could have caused such an illogical skew.

Law school was like military boot camp, preparing legal warriors using mostly the Socratic Method, hierarchy, power techniques (humiliation) and even bluffing (non-truth) as an accepted tactic to win. Students were pitted against each other to such extent that some of them cut pages out of the library books to make sure that no one else would be able to complete our assignments. Only a certain percentage of students could get high grades, which meant that some had to get low grades, regardless. The professors created a culture of fear and competition, where everyone was expected to behave as "gentlemen." Our diplomas were printed in Latin, a language that none of my clients speaks and no one can read. When I asked if I could have a diploma in English, the "School" informed me that this was not possible, because it was a tradition to print it in

Latin (a tradition of elitism in my opinion). I was miserable, and my whole body broke out in a rash within six months. Who made *this* game up?

When I revealed the gender skew to the press, hoping that bringing it to the school's attention would open a conversation, I was portrayed as a radical feminist. The president of the college villainized me rather than addressing the real issues. This is a typical reaction within a fearful framework.

I share stories such as this in hopes that it will inspire all of us, men and women, to begin to notice and question the norms of our culture with an eye toward creating a world that reflects who we REALLY are, rather than one of fear and power struggle.

Whose game are you playing? Who wrote the rules? How is it working for you?

# Day 2:

. . . . . . . . . . . . . . . . .

## Commune with Nature

## AFFIRMATION:

*"As I commune with Nature, I am healed."*

What in nature calls to you? Are you renewed when you go to the mountaintop, the forest, the desert, the ocean, the rivers, or to waterfalls? ***Go there,*** even if only in your mind. Find your sanctuary in the elements; this earth was created to heal you. It calls you for a reason. Breathe deeply there, letting it all in. Let it strengthen you. How can you commune with nature on a daily basis? Can you go for a walk in a garden? Can you go to the beach? This is your peaceful place, where you can return at any moment in which you need to feel centered again. Find your sanctuary! Receive nature's gift of peace and healing. Let the sunshine in or feel the rain soaking into your skin. Both want to touch your skin in adoration.

"Forget not that the wind loves to feel your hair, and the earth longs to feel your feet."[xv]

The green of the earth and the gold of the sunlight infuse you, both physically and spiritually, with the frequency of fresh air and invigoration. The plants and flowers cheerfully long to raise your frequency with their essential gifts. Buy some flowers or make an herbal tea to rejoice!

Once you find yourself in your peaceful place, soften your vision and ask for a plant, animal, rock or element of nature to make itself known to you as an ally. Bring your loving focus to it. Cherish and adore it. Listen to it with deep curiosity. Be quiet. Let it speak to you.

When I first did this exercise, I came upon a dandelion, never before had I appreciated how brilliant these plants are. In fact, I had always considered them weeds and pulled them out of my garden. After the dandelion and I communed for about twenty minutes, I learned three lessons:

## Lesson 1:

The Dandelion called to me with its cheerful yellow flower and asked me to eat its leaf. It taught me that its leaf is just what I needed to help my sugar cravings. It could support my body's need to create more red blood cells, without which I feel tired.

## Lesson 2:

Dandelions are the most magical flowers. They are the only flower that grants wishes. You simply blow their seeds to the wind while making a wish and expect your intention to come true, as the seeds plant themselves everywhere. This, in turn, creates more dandelions, and the capacity for wish-granting multiplies exponentially. It' as if a Genie in a bottle asked you for your third wish and you replied 1000 more wishes. This was a lesson in abundance and magical thinking.

## Lesson 3:

Dandelions are very hearty and robust. This type had some prickly parts to discourage animals from eating it. I had never allowed myself to have prickly parts before because they weren't "nice." Growing up, the expectation was that girls were nice and smiled. In the past, I would let people bulldoze over me, because, in trying to be nice, I had no boundaries. I would end up feeling depleted and resentful. This little dandelion taught me to value boundaries, even if they're prickly.

In our busy urban culture, we must take time to commune with nature to remember ourselves as a part of it. If we don't know ourselves, we are just going through the motions of what we think we "should" do, rather than what we "came here" to do. As a daily ritual, I go to the ocean, jump in, and let the wind, the water, and the sunshine remind me who I really am. Find your happy place and go there frequently.

# Day 3:

. . . . . . . . . . . . . . . . .

## Setting your Intentions

## AFFIRMATION:

*"I know what I want, and I gratefully receive it. I let go of needing to know HOW my desires will come to me."*

It's no coincidence that Artemis (the Greek Goddess) and Katniss (from the Hunger Games[xvi]) were both known for their aim with a bow and arrow. The bow and arrow are one powerful archetype. They are a metaphor for the power of focused intention. The idea is that you:

- ♥ **KNOW YOUR GOAL.**

- ♥ **AIM FOR IT.**

- ♥ **PRACTICE PERSISTENTLY,** and you will hit your target.

The same is true when creating anything, for example, a new habit. We must first know what we desire. Second, we must take aim—do something even if it's just visualizing your goal. Third, keep trying until we arrive at our destination.

We can't set intentions until we actually come to know what we want. **What do you want?** That's not as easy as it sounds for most women. We are often so busy trying to take care of everyone else that it doesn't even occur to us to want something. Start with the easy stuff, like, "I want to feel healthy and vibrant"—"I want to feel beautiful in my body"—"I want more joy and laughter." Take some time to get in touch with what you REALLY want. You can also discover what you DO want by knowing what you DON'T want. For example, maybe you are feeling depleted in a current relationship. By recognizing that you feel depleted, you realize that you want a fulfilling relationship where your partner contributes to you. Knowing what you DON'T want also helps you to identify aspects of a relationship that would be a "deal breaker." I may desire one-hundred things in a partner but only 20 are deal breakers. If I focus on getting the deal breakers satisfied during the first date, then I will know if a second date is a waste of time. Whatever you identify as your desire, be as specific as you can. Don't just desire a new job. Ask for your dream job. Maybe you want to be an astronaut that discovers a new planet.

*Setting intentions* is the aim that an archer takes. It is the most powerful step. Until you let the arrow go in the direction of your dreams, the universe doesn't know what you're aiming for. You must take some kind of action. Action may be as simple as visioning your dream, asking the universe for what you want or cutting out a picture for your vision board. It may be a verbal declaration witnessed by another. For example, declare, "I am totally free, happy and healthy now and forever," or "I am a money magnet." Take time to journal your intentions today.

*Whatever action you feel truly inspired to take, take it.* It's especially exciting when your step is "full-on" and shows your commitment. By that, I mean there is no going back. For example, when I wrote a letter to all of my clients letting them know that I would be moving to Hawaii, there was no taking that announcement back. You might need to purchase an airline ticket, buy a web domain for your new business, or finally come "out of the closet." Just take one-step! Shoot for the moon. The more you are all in; the more likely you are to succeed.

The last step after you take aim is to let the arrow go! *You must let go* of your preconceived ideas of how your arrow will reach its target. Let the universe handle this last bit. Don't try to control HOW it flies after you've let your arrow go, as long as your desire is realized. For example, gifts may come in unexpected packages or from unforeseen sources.

I'm sure you've heard about the man in a flood, standing on the roof of his house engulfed by water. He prayed and believed that God would save him. A boat came by and offered to rescue him. The man said, "No thanks, God will save me." Then a helicopter came, and he again said, "No thanks, God will save me." After he drowned and went to heaven, he asked God why he had not saved him. God said, "What more do you want? I sent a boat and a helicopter!"[xvii] Let go of how your lifeboat might look and let others contribute to you. The more you practice archery with your life, the more often you will hit your target!

# Day 4:

· · · · · · · · · · · · · · · · · ·

## The Marriage Within

## VOW:

*"I am whole and complete. I hereby vow to love and adore myself unconditionally, forever. I vow to listen to and honor my truth. I vow to gratefully care for my body, mind, and spirit."*

If you haven't already married yourself, today is your wedding day! It's time to realize and ritualize the truth of your completeness. There is no one else outside of you that can complete you. You are it!

You are both masculine AND feminine, creating a powerful balance of tools in your toolbox to use as you choose.

Our outer relationships are only as good as the person we bring to them. If we bring only a part of ourselves, looking for someone else to complete us, we will sabotage that relationship out of "neediness"—unless, of course, you find an enabler who wants to keep you small. I can relate to that approach, having lived it, but I do not recommend it.

That's not to say we can't lean on each other in an interdependent way, but leaning-in is a choice, not a chronic emotional need. Relationships with others should feel like a bouquet of flowers. Flowers add diversity, richness, and beauty to our lives, but they are not necessary for our survival. Like flowers, we can bring our whole self to our relationships. The stronger we are as individuals, the stronger our relationships can be.

We carry all that we need inside of us if we just stopped to notice. I know that this can be hard to believe because all the marketing around us tells us that we need something more to be happy or complete. I remember when I used to think, "If I just had prettier clothes," or "If I just had a perfect boyfriend," then everything would be OK. It can take some soul searching to realize finally that you are more than enough just as you are. In the meantime, let's fake it, and simply declare it so. The universe loves to play along with our games.

Your inner marriage may be as simple as saying the affirmation to yourself. Feel free to rewrite your vows. You may want to wear a particular ring to symbolize your commitment to yourself. You may want to wear a specific color or put on your favorite music. Make this marriage befitting your station – noble if that is what you need. Some of us need to take things more lightly and may prefer to marry ourselves while hula hooping in the rain, for example. You won't forget that moment! Whatever you decide, it should be meaningful to you. We are meaning-making machines, so create something good.

You may want to have witnesses present. Let's call this a party. Feel free to have one! You can send out invitations and even register to honor your inner marriage. This is where your inner masculine and feminine are both acknowledged and agree to work together. Sharing our spiritual victories with others makes them more real, and it invites others to help us remember whom we really are, in case we forget.

If this all sounds silly to you, then take a moment to get in touch with how your life might have been different in the past had you recognized your completeness, and realized that there was nothing, emotionally and spiritually, you needed outside of yourself. Most of us spend a lot of time and money trying to fill up a void, especially with food, relationships, shopping, overworking, or other addictive behaviors. Does that sound familiar? Have fun with this–weddings are joyful.

# Day 5:

. . . . . . . . . . . . . . . . .

## Abundance

## AFFIRMATION:

*"I am full now. I am totally fulfilled and completely satisfied. All I need and want is already within me. Thank you!"*

Abundance is similar to happiness. It's not a place to "arrive." It's a result of an abundant state of mind. It's a choice. You can have the experience of abundance NOW, regardless of your circumstances. By living in your current abundance, you will attract even more abundance. The good news is that you are already there—you already have abundance. If you don't feel that's true for you, then please repeat the gratitude exercise on Day 7 of Step 4.

Abundance is the sense that there is plenty for everyone, that we *can* all have it all. This sense follows naturally for those who trust in the universe to provide. As a child, I did not have this trust because I experienced my world from scarcity. In spite of my past experience, today, I *choose* to trust. There are three reasons:

1. It feels better than fear.

2. It's true at least on a spiritual level in that I receive exactly what I need for my spiritual evolution, including the challenges.

3. If I generate trust, it is more likely to show up in my life. I create my perception of reality.

Ask yourself where you experience a sense of "not enough." Is it money, love or intimacy? Is it respect? Is it fun? When you feel "not enough," you have created a story of scarcity, and you are not alone. Most of the world is conspiring against you. Journal about your experience of "not enough." Where do you tell that story? What price do you pay? What do you get out of it—what's your payoff? How is it working for you?

Let's take my personal favorite: *"not enough time"* for example. I asked myself "Where did this story come from, and how did it serve me?" This old story stopped me from having richer relationships with friends and family. When I was with others, I listened to their stories, usually disempowering ones. As an empath, I felt their emotions, the injustice, the victim, their anger. Without training in how to maintain my own emotional boundaries, this kind of listening left me feeling depleted, especially when I didn't "have enough time" to take care of myself. I often become resentful that MY needs weren't met and inevitably blamed my conversation partner for talking my ear off. Thus, I avoided conversations and avoided people. My unconscious strategy was to fill up my calendar so much that I didn't have enough time for friends and family. That way, I could just say, "I'm too busy" instead of, "I don't want to talk to you," thereby risking hurting someone's feelings.

I used food the same way at parties sometimes. I would go right for the buffet, focusing on something OTHER than talking to people. It felt safer because food wouldn't speak to me or judge me.

When I tell myself there's "not enough time" to take care of myself, such as preparing healthy meals or exercising, it's just an excuse to avoid responsibility for my own care. I would never say that I didn't have enough time to feed my children or walk my dog! Yet I seem to have no problem saying that to myself. I seem to resent how much time it takes to care for my body, as though it's unreasonably "high maintenance." The truth is the deferred maintenance catches up with me, leaving me overwhelmed by the need to catch up with its basic care. Inevitably, I find myself cutting corners and reaching for processed food snacks and sugar again.

If I gave myself permission to be treated like the precious being that I am, with the kind of care that befits who I really am, I would undoubtedly prioritize eating well and exercising myself by walking, because I'm worth it. If that's the case, then my story about "not enough time" was just a convenient excuse to avoid other people. The truth is we make time for what we want most.

What if instead of blaming time, I learned to speak my truth?

What if I could lovingly say something like:

♥ *"Thank you for the invitation to lunch, and I've decided to take time today for rest and self-care."*

♥ *"I would love to spend time with you, and right now I need to go into my chrysalis so I can come out a butterfly. I'm taking a break for a while. I have no idea when I might emerge. Can we talk after that?"*

♥ *"I'm making my health my priority right now, and that means I'm not adding any social events to my calendar at the moment. I'll let you know when that changes."*

What if I learned to protect my emotional boundaries? Then, when I choose to listen, I would be uplifted instead of upset. Depending on the context and the strength of the relationship, I could say something like:

♥ *"Thank you for sharing what's up in our life. I really want to know you better, AND your story triggers my own emotions. I'm not sure how to maintain my own well-being right now except to take a break from this conversation. Can we talk again later, when my emotions have dissipated?"*

♥ *"I feel you—that's a very sad story. I understand that you may be grieving. Would you be interested in sharing uplifting stories as well? Like, what are you passionate about in life? What spiritual victories have you experienced recently?"*

♥ *"I'm trying to take more time for self-care, like meditation, naps and hot baths. I think I need to take a little time to myself right now. Please excuse me."*

♥ *"I enjoy being with you, and I sometimes get overwhelmed by all the talking I do all day. Could we do something that doesn't involve talking, like taking a walk or watching one of our favorite movies together?"*

Old habits can be hard to break until we get in touch with the price we really pay for them. When I pretend that there is not enough time, I find myself limited in:

- ♥ **LOVE AND CONNECTION.** This affects how many friends I can have, and the depth of the emotional intimacy available. I find that I don't spend as much time as I'd like with my family.

- ♥ **MY LEVEL OF HEALTH AND VITALITY.** I seldom give myself enough time to prepare nutritious food, exercise, and rest or have a rich spiritual life, all of which are basic ingredients for vital energy.

- ♥ **PLAYTIME—JOY.** I don't let myself spend time playing when there is so much work to do is in so little time.

- ♥ **WHAT I CAN ACCOMPLISH.** When I take a moment to write down all the contributions, I would love to make to this world, if time were not a limiting factor, there is a very long list! It's not unlike the exercise we did previously when we won the lottery, and money was unlimited.

If you are like me, you're thinking, "But time IS limited!" "We only have an average of 85 years on this planet if we're born into privilege!" You say it like time is real. You believe it's real because we have all decided that it's a useful concept for physics, science, making appointments and organizing society. It also gives us a structure that our brains are wired to understand. How convenient. How limiting.

Just for today, let's play with the idea that linear time is just a convenient story we made up for the purposes mentioned above. Assume that it is really just an illusion, like daylight savings time. Then assume that there is no beginning or end—that the past, present, and future are all happening at once.

Don't try to wrap your mind around this new possibility or understand it, since our brains aren't wired for this. Instead, just decide it. Choose it, for now, to see what happens in timelessness. How would your world be different outside of the time constraint? What choices would be accessible to you that are not currently available? Who would guide you through this unknown time warp?

Try moving forward in time and asking your future Self a question, like, "What is a wise question I might ask my Future Self that would make a difference in 'the now'?" Try moving back to your past and reinvent it. Yes, this is time travel—in your mind. Your mind will not know the difference if YOU do not. I won't tell.

I could reinvent my entire childhood from here as though I've turned back time and relived it. I could change one pivotal moment and rewrite my own history in a way that improves my future. For example, my father left when I was three-years-old. At the time, I decided there was something wrong with me. Going back in time in my mind, I reimagine that moment of daddy's leaving and in three-year-old words, insert an antidote to that old story. My wise Self-injects:

"Daddy needed a timeout to heal his broken heart, and he was very wise to listen. That timeout made it possible for him to be the best Daddy he could be for me later. I know so many people who die from broken hearts. It would be a good thing if everyone listened to what they needed to heal and had space to do so."

I just now made that up. How simple that was, and I feel so much lighter somehow. It's such a beautiful new story. Instead of believing Daddy was wrong—therefore all men are wrong—for leaving their families, I honor his needs, his process, and his contribution. At this moment, I believe that healthy men don't just leave their families without good reason. I now choose to give them the benefit of the doubt. The best part is that I don't make it about ME anymore. It never was. I've spent my entire life afraid that men would leave me. In turn, I did not allow myself to trust or depend on them. This belief became a self-fulfilling prophecy – one I choose not to hold any longer. It does not serve me. Thank you for witnessing. It is done.

Healing the past and retrieving wisdom from the future is available to all of us outside of our perceptions of time. Try time travel for yourself.

# Day 6:

. . . . . . . . . . . . . . . . . .

## Perfectionism

## AFFIRMATION:

*"I am perfect right now, just as I am at this moment. I always was and always will be."*

Was it hard to say that affirmation? Assuming it is actually true; ask yourself, "How can that statement be true?"

When I remember that I'm a spiritual being having a human experience, I recall that my soul is unaffected by disease, by emotions, or by circumstances. I've seen images taken by a Kirlian camera of a torn leaf.[7] The camera takes photos of the essence of the leaf, its energy or light body. Although a portion of the leaf was missing in the physical realm, it was complete and whole in the photograph. That's what we are like—always perfect in the spiritual sense.

---

[7] *https://en.wikipedia.org/wiki/Kirlian_photography*

When we remember our true selves, we realize that this body will come and go, but we are eternal.

Our physicality does not limit our essential selves.

I've heard about a tribe in Africa[xviii] that makes it their job to remind someone lovingly **who they really are** after they have committed a crime. Instead of punishment, they assume that a murderer or thief has temporarily forgotten who he or she really is. The tribe places the perpetrator in the center of the circle for as long as it takes to remind him or her by retelling their life story from the perspective of their wholeness, not their brokenness, from their connection to their community, not their isolation. The tribe sees the perpetrator in his/her perfection, strength and beauty, not in their short-fallings.

It's time to let perfectionism go! It only gets in our way. When faced with an opportunity, I used to say, "I'm not ready," which really meant, "I'm not perfect enough or good enough." Initially, I thought that I had to overcome my food addiction before I could write this book and share it with the world. At that rate, I might never be ready! That stopped me for years.

We are forever in process, individually and collectively. If we assume there is plenty of time, we wait for perfection because there is no hurry in eternity. As my mother used to say, "God isn't finished with me yet." Be gentle with yourself. When you're not, others feel imperfect too.

I once invited a woman to come to one of my mermaid retreats. She said, "I'm too fat to be a mermaid." I talked her into coming anyway. She soon discovered that mermaids—like humans—come in all sizes, shapes, and colors. From there, she had the courage to open that portal of possibility and has been playing mermaid with me ever since.

How has your own perfectionism stopped you? What if you were unstoppable? What if the idea of perfection was less powerful than a vulnerability in accomplishing the same goals?

# Day 7:

## Workaholism

## AFFIRMATION:

*"I am more than enough, worthy and precious, just by being here. There is nowhere to go and nothing to get."*

Like most addictions, working too much or too hard is just another way to avoid feelings or dealing with what's real. It's just so much more acceptable in our culture to be a workaholic than to be a drug addict—in fact, workaholics are often rewarded with praises, promotions, and bonuses for productivity. The harder I worked, the more money I made, and the more money I made, the more I thought I might feel safe from scarcity. This was an illusion.

The experience of scarcity or abundance is a state of being, not based on how much money one has. If you don't believe me, pretend that you have one million dollars cash and ask yourself how to invest it. Fear of losing it tends to seep in when scarcity is our past patterning, whether investing in the stock market, starting your own business or sharing with others.

Driven by the story of "not enough," we find ourselves in a vicious consumer cycle that encourages us to spend now and pay later to buy all the things we learned to want. The average United States household income in 2016 was $59,039.[xix] Our personal debt in the United States averages $131,431 per person (This includes credit cards, auto loan, mortgages and student loans.) of which $15,654 is from credit card debt.[xx] With credit card interest rates, no wonder we have to work so hard to keep up with our bills. Our work can feel like a golden cage and limit our freedom.

For those of us who grew up with the Puritan "work hard" ethic, we have a life-long value system to overcome unless we want our lives to be "hard." Our economy relies on worker bees and wants us to stay that way. Giving up an old belief system leaves a vacuum that requires a new one to fill it. Create something new like "my play can be my work." Maybe you've always wanted to be an artist or a toy designer or an actress. These can also be "work." We are only limited by our thinking. Open up to "anything is possible" and imagine work that you would enjoy even if you weren't paid for it.

You may have noticed that instead of focusing on the problem, addiction, we are focusing your attention on what you want in life and your joy. If you find what truly fulfills you, you will stop trying to fill yourself with things that don't serve you. Problems resolve themselves when we are in alignment with who we really are![8]

There is one more reason I became a workaholic. I wanted to

---

[8] This can even apply to cancer. I suggest that you read, Anita Moorjani, Dying To Be Me, (Carlsbad, California, Hay House, 2012).

feel important. I thought that if I really worked hard, then I would accomplish something great, contribute something significant to humanity and feel valuable. This is normal for the human ego. It's just a symptom of lack of self-esteem—a forgetfulness that I am already important in a spiritual sense.

It is genuinely enough just to be me, present and fully self-expressed. I can do nothing to make my higher power love me more or love me less. I am loved unconditionally whether I end up in a position of power or not. Let this in, while taking a moment. Most of us grew up thinking love was conditional. To think that we can be valuable, regardless of our behavior, can be a radical shift in our belief system. This shift creates a core sense of value that will be a springboard to freedom if you choose to let it in.

Journal about how you would experience life differently if you didn't have to DO anything to be worthy of love. Are you climbing the corporate ladder of someone else's dream? Are you working three jobs so you can support your children's expectations for a middle-class lifestyle? Are you sacrificing your well-being for others and feeling resentful about it?

Journal about the price you are paying for working too much, too hard or in the wrong field. We won't feel motivated to give something up until we are genuinely in touch with the price we pay for it. In my case, my health and vitality are depleted leaving me utterly exhausted. I don't have time or energy for relationships or for a sex drive. The worst part is that I never seem to have time to play or be creative—the whole reason I came to this planet in the first place! What did you come here for?

# STEP 6:

............

*Inspiration*

# Day 1:

. . . . . . . . . . . . . . . . .

## Inspiration through Breath

## AFFIRMATION:

*"I allow Divine inspiration to flow through me like a river of endless light. I breathe deeply into all that I am."*

Believe me, the Divine light flows through your veins and makes up every molecule of your being. It is our job to:

- ♥ **NOTICE THIS FLOW.**

- ♥ **SHARE THESE GIFTS.**

- ♥ **REMOVE ANY OBSTACLES FROM ITS FLOW.**

Truth is usually straightforward. Inspiration is the breath of the Divine flowing through you. Enthusiasm is the breath of life. The Breath is everything!

Hawaiian tradition begins with "Aloha." The "ha" in Aloha means the breath of life—the same breath that created humanity in Judeo-Christian tradition. When foreigners first arrived in Hawaii, the Hawaiians called them "haole." This word meant that they had no breath of life and they did not breathe into their prayers, as Hawaiians traditionally do, to empower them.

In Western culture, we have forgotten the power and importance of the breath of life. The breath as a spiritual practice is the basis of Yoga and many other breathing practices. Take a few deep breaths as often as you can, particularly when accessing your inspiration. Making time for inspiration is also required to access your greatest gifts.

Today, remember to breathe deeply.

# Day 2:

. . . . . . . . . . . . . . . . .

## Acknowledging Your Gifts and Talents

### AFFIRMATION:

*"I carry many gifts and talents with me, and I'm inspired to share them."*

It's time to acknowledge the gifts and talents that you bring to this world because they are where you'll find your inspiration to contribute. In your contribution, you will find your greatest joy, and in your greatest joy, addictive habits will often disappear themselves.

If you already know what your gifts and talents are, make a list of them. If you're not sure, try asking people who love you and try this exercise to help you remember:[9]

Write out a timeline of your major life events. You were shaped by these core events. By that I mean, you had an emotional reaction to them, made up a story, and that story became a belief that shaped

---

[9] *I learned this exercise from a Glowshop offered by Katie Macks at http://katiemacks.com, 2015.*

how you perceived reality. Often these stories are either traumatic or ecstatic and from them emerge our gifts and talents. Now that you have your own list of events add the spiritual qualities that you acquired at each point. For example, here are some of mine...

| Event | Gifts/Talents I discovered |
|---|---|
| Age 0: I was born to loving parents | Love, spiritual base |
| Age 3: Father left family | Self-reliance, entrepreneur |
| Age 4: I went to school | Intelligence and kindness to others |
| Age 5: I played "doctor" with the neighbor boy and felt ashamed | Passion for sex education, women's issues, and compassion |
| Age 6: Sister was born | Caring for others, responsibility |
| Age 10: I went to summer camp | Fun, play, courage & humor |
| Age 13: Worked with my father in his doctor office | Healing is a spiritual process and wisdom |
| Age 19: Lived in Istanbul, Turkey 1 year | Curiosity, adventure, cross-cultural awareness, women's issue |
| Age 25: Law School | Writing and playing the legal "game," politics and self-defense |
| Age 35: Met my fairy godmother | I'm a mermaid! |

Aside from identifying our gifts and talents, the other benefit of this exercise is to appreciate how adverse events (such as trauma) can often be our greatest teachers.

Now, you should have a list of several gifts and talents that you bring to this world. Prioritize the ones you enjoy sharing the most by circling the ones that light you up the most. These are the most accessible to you because they inspire you, so focus on cultivating those gifts and talents first.

Your life-long homework is to bring your gifts and talents fully to the world. This is your authentic Self-expression! Maybe you are a singer, a poet or a dancer, and you haven't given yourself enough space to share these parts of yourself. Perhaps you've always had a passion for making fairy gardens, or you've always wanted to be a doctor. **Start today!** I know there is a fountain maker inside of me waiting to come out and play! Our culture does not monetarily reward some of our most inspirational gifts and talents. They are not what our culture considers valuable, so rewards are not as consistent as being a lawyer, for example. That's how I ended up unhappy, bewildered and reaching for food to comfort myself. How did you end up reaching for food?

# Day 3:

. . . . . . . . . . . . . . . . . .

## Focus on Your Life Purpose

## AFFIRMATION:

*"My rich life experiences have prepared me well to contribute to others."*

My greatest joy flows from contributing my gifts and talents to others in alignment with my purpose. It's funny that during the twenty four years I spent in formal school, no one ever asked the question, "What is your life purpose." It seems like a fundamental question to me. At the same time, I notice a little bit of resistance to asking myself that question. Are you feeling that too? For me, it's like a fear that I'll discover that the Divine purpose is not in alignment with my personal agenda. This is a higher Self vs. little Self-conversation. My higher Self-says, "I'm here to be physically healthy to accomplish my purpose," and my little self-says, "But I want to eat the entire chocolate cake." Does this sound familiar? Maybe my higher Self-says, "You are here, to be honest, and courageous," and my little self-says, "But it's much more comfortable to play small and hide in my food."

Begin to notice what your inner conversations are. If they ask— "What is my life purpose?—answer the question.

If you are already clear about your life's purpose, congratulations, you are halfway there. Now all you have to do is focus your attention on it. If you are clear, you can skip to the discussion on next page.

If, like most people, you are not sure what your life purpose is, here's an exercise to help:

For this inquiry, assume the following:

- ♥ All of the life experiences you have created thus far are your training to fulfill your purpose. There are no mistakes. Each event, traumatic or blissful, occurred for a reason.

- ♥ All of the gifts and talents you have acquired along the way were specifically given to support your purpose. (Refer to the Day 2 list you made previously in Step 6) Do you see any patterns?

- ♥ *Your deepest joy will reveal your Divine purpose.* Follow your joy. What really lights you up without effort? I have to think hard to determine why I find joy in eating an entire chocolate cake—it represents a more profound desire for more sweetness and delight in my life. These qualities are part of why I am here. We can find sweetness and delight in a warm bath, laughing at a good joke or indulging in a sweet friendship, which brings emotional intimacy.

♥ **As you continue to develop, your purpose is likely to change.** Don't worry, that's how humans work. It's your Spirit moving you; it's normal and means your purpose is not set in stone. So relax and write down a purpose that works for you today. Update it as the Spirit moves you.

On one level, we are all here to accomplish the same purpose because we are all one, which, in my opinion, is to **love more deeply than we ever knew possible**. I believe that we all came from a heavenly realm initially, a dimension where it's effortless to love everyone, and the bigger picture is clearer. I believe we came to this planet to see if we could generate love even in the face of adversity. The more challenging our world becomes, the more opportunity we have to dive deeper into love—beyond rational, logical thought. On a spiritual level, it's like having a final exam. Rarely are exams considered fun, but they do test our mastery. The harder the exam, the more amazed we are when we pass the test. If we are here to obtain our "black belt" in love and other Divine qualities, then the universe will conspire to support us by testing us along the way.

To focus our attention on our specific purpose(s) allows us, on a more personal level, to become more aware of them and creates heaven on earth. If we fail to connect to our higher purpose, we either live a benign life of emptiness or worse, create havoc. For example, consider Adolph Hitler who believed he was making the world a better place—he was limited by who he believed would be included in his concept of heaven on Earth. His personal agenda was fear-based rather than connected to his higher Self or love-based.

Fortunately, humanity is evolving. Ancient wisdom and modern philosophy both suggest that we are making a leap right now from the third dimension to the fifth dimension.[xxi] Don't worry that doesn't require leaving this planet. *It requires that we wake up to our purpose and focus on it.*

If you would like to see what I've come up with so far, check out my purpose in Exhibit E. I read this every morning and focus my attention on it throughout the day. I visualize myself in my purpose and make decisions in alignment with it. My purpose is an authentic expression of who I am and why I'm here. So far, I've only tapped into the tip of the iceberg—I can't wait to see what unfolds next—for all of us!

# Day 4:

. . . . . . . . . . . . . . . . . .

## Effervescent Fluidity & Spontaneity

## AFFIRMATION:

*"Life is a dance in which I flow freely and gracefully. I am strong and easy going, spontaneous and fluid, flexible and fun."*

Rigidity is a tool to protect us from threats. The more rigidly we hold onto our beliefs, the safer we feel. Rigid beliefs indicate a need for more trust and less fear. I have high compassion for those who hold rigid beliefs because it soon becomes a prison.

I can't tell you how many times I have started a rigid diet only to feel tyrannized by it in the end. It is the opposite of freedom and immediately triggers a desire to rebel inside of me. Notice how turtle shells have evolved for their protection, but in exchange, turtles now lack mobility. Personally, I would rather live one day free than a lifetime in prison. I would rather be a delicate rose in full bloom than a three hundred-year-old tortoise. If you had to choose between freedom of mobility and a chronic protective shell, which would you prefer?

So how do we get in touch with our spontaneous, effervescent fluidity? It helps to get moving from our power source. That's why mermaids say, "Go with the flow." Mermaids undulate their bodies to propel themselves. It's like a constantly flowing moving dance. They learn from the waves, the seaweed, and the dolphins. The power in the mermaid stroke is at the core of their body—like a Pilates class. It also, coincidentally, comes from the second chakra—the energy center that is the home of their creativity, their womb, and their passion. This is a powerful place to flow from and to move. If you don't have a swimming tail, take a belly dance class to get the same motion going.

You may have noticed that when men walk, this second chakra area usually leads them, and their body follows. Picture John Wayne and try walking with your hips forward. Women, in my experience, typically lead with their head instead. If you saw a woman walk with her womb leading the way, you might think she was audacious and bold. We women often kick our passion and creativity to the back of the bus, in favor of our endless "to do" list-which resides in our heads as we set out to accomplish daily tasks. Try walking with different parts of your body in the lead to see how it feels.

Getting in touch with our spontaneous flow may require us to get out of our own way. We have to get out of our heads, out of our limited thinking and out of our daily habits, such as morning coffee, news, work, etc. What would it be like if you created space in your calendar to let your joy bubble up effortlessly? Would your life be different if more often you just "went with the flow"?

I tried this out recently. One of my greatest joys is making others laugh. Until a week ago, I thought I had to prepare and memorize a script and a sit-down-comedy[10] routine to make this possible. I was afraid I would flop, and self-consciousness kept me from performing. Finally, I chose to set aside those limiting beliefs, and with a group of friends, in a supportive container, I allowed them to create my comic persona by projecting onto me what they wanted to see. Spontaneously, a character that had never existed before was born with their input. I ended up speaking only out of the left side of my mouth with an English accent, like a small child spouting ridiculous wisdom in answer to their various "deep" questions. The experience was delightfully interactive and hysterically funny to all of us.

What if I applied this same wisdom to food? How could food choices be more spontaneous? Would that make eating more joyful and less of a burden?

My inner grown-up has been telling my inner child what is "good" and "bad" food my whole life, and it just isn't fun enough. It feels like I'm always in trouble with my inner critique for wanting to eat a peanut butter and jelly sandwich on white bread! Grown-up food doesn't always taste good and doesn't really excite me because it's just so responsible—remember, I was an overly responsible child. What if, instead, I let my inner child lead the way within the framework of the "healthy pantry?" I would only stock food or ingredients that are "healthy" from my adult perspective, but my creative, playful, fun three-year-old would prepare it! In the past, I avoided food preparation but now cannot wait to see what my inner child comes up with next. I'll be sure to take a photo and share it on Facebook.

---

[10] *Mermaids cannot stand-up in their tails, so I have to sit.*

This will help me remember the "joy" of cooking, inspire others and encourage them to share their fun recipes as well. What inspires YOU?

# Day 5:

. . . . . . . . . . . . . . . . . .

## Creativity is the new Currency [11]

## AFFIRMATION:

*"I am a magnet for creative ideas. They flow through me like white water rapids, playfully dancing through my life with joy."*

Creativity is a Divine gift, as is grace. We all have the capacity to create something novel if we are willing to allow the Divine to make us be a fountain of flowing delight. Creativity comes *through* us, not from us. It is like birthing something new into the world, even if it is just a fresh look at something old. It flows from "nothing," and no matter how much we try, we cannot force it into existence using our conscious will. There are, however, steps we can take to encourage the flow.

Since I live on the Big Island of Hawaii, I like to visualize my creativity as hot lava flowing gently from the top of the mountain into the sea. It is a constant glowing, gentle flow and requires me to get

---

[11] *Lori Solay, who is a Conscious Creativity Catalyst, Certified Hypnotherapist, NLP Master Practitioner can be found at https://www.facebook.com/solaycreative.*

out of the way. You may prefer a more explosive metaphor like fireworks, or perhaps you are more of a river person. Choose whatever works for you.

I am using metaphor because we are seeking to access the subconscious rather than the conscious mind. The conscious mind is where we already think we know something, and our intelligence can get in the way of novel ideas. The subconscious mind, however, is where we have access to all the information we do not know consciously. What's really fun is that we don't even know that we do not know it, but that part of us is connected to all the knowing. This is the part we want to access—the parts of yourself you have not yet met yet. This will allow you to discover the gifts and talents that you didn't even know you had.

Imagine your Self as a being of light that is about 350 feet high. Now, consider that you're trying to fit that massive soul into a little walking sack of salt water held together by skin, such that it doesn't leak and there are a few bones for structural mobility, i.e., your physical body. You are aware of the first five or six feet of your existence, which is your body, but you still have another three-hundred-forty-four feet of your Self to explore and get to know. To access these lesser-known parts of yourself, draw on paper some circles inside the three hundred fiftyfoot column of light. I call this the "Bubble Theory of Self" because if you draw it on paper, it looks like a bag of bubbles awaiting discovery.

One small bubble makes up who I am in the bigger picture. This Bubble might be a mermaid, a lawyer, an angel, an artist, a writer, a daughter, a dragon or a fifth-dimensional cosmic cheerleader—whatever that is. Since you may not have met the other parts of you yet, fill in the bubbles with features you want to explore, so you can find out what, if any, part of that bubble is authentic for you.

For example, in my case, the mermaid bubble is more real than the lawyer bubble in my drawing of my Self. The prosthetic tail I wear to swim in is not "real"—so that part of being a mermaid is not authentic. When children ask me if I'm a real mermaid, I can honestly answer, "Yes," and explain that I was born with a disability, legs.

The purpose of drawing your Self this way is to provide a sense of self that is much bigger than may have previously imagined. You can explore your Self playfully with this map. In this model, the more a small bubble concept fits into your larger Self, the more authentic it is for you. As the small bubble falls more outside of your larger Self, the roles you play become more important than your larger Self, much like wearing a costume becomes a role. The goal of using this theory is to figure out what parts of your Self-are your most authentic expression, and stop worrying about the stuff that falls outside your authentic bubble. Just because I'm a mermaid doesn't mean I have to be born with a physical tail, for example—that has nothing to do with the gifts and talents I bring. How will YOU know the difference? You'll have to play the role and try it on. Your "feeling navigator" will tell you what's real.

One of the most critical skills we must master to play this game is "feeling navigation." It's the only way to know what's "real" when we are outside of the known. Whenever I experience truth, I get a chill that shoots up my spine. Some people are auditory and hear the "ring" of truth. Some of us are visual and see a "spark" of truth. How does your body let you know when you've discovered something real?

Now, try playing with all those bubbles you drew inside of your Self-bubble. Try them on. Embody them. Remember when you were a child, and pretended to be something else? Maybe you liked to play house and played "mom," "dad" or the "child" to see what that would be like. We must get out of the known to discover the unknown. Have fun with this! Every man I know wore a superhero cape as a child. Try to remember what you dreamed of being as a child – there's usually some truth to it.

Aside from playing, you can take **other steps to access your creative flow.** For example, to write the first draft of these 13 Steps, I awaken in the dark at 5 am every morning because my conscious mind has not really kicked in yet. I don't turn lights on because I want to stay in that partly sleepy mode left over from my dream time. I get out of my own way as much as possible, writing that which feels inspiring to my personal journey, hoping it may also assist others. I try not to think about anything. At this time of the morning, all is quiet except for the birds in the garden. It reminds me of a whirling dervish, dancing in a circle to achieve a trance state. Do whatever it takes to get out of the part of yourself that thinks it already knows everything there is to know.

If you want the universe to surprise and delight you, then you must get out of the known and be open to the unknown, the currently unseen world. I've heard that when Christopher Columbus landed in the Americas, the native people asked him how he had arrived there. He pointed to his ships on the horizon and said, "By ship." At first, the natives were unable to see the ships because they had no reference for ships, never having seen one before. I believe there is much we do not see. Widen your awareness by playing awareness games. Begin to look at things as if you've never seen them before. Begin to taste things as if you've never tasted them before. Use your peripheral vision the next time you go for a walk by softening your normal vision. For example, I'll send an awareness prize to any reader who can tell me how many times I use the word "bubble" in this book.

Creativity requires spaciousness. You must give yourself the luxury of daydreaming or just time to putter. Creative ideas emerge when we are not looking for them because we are not looking in our brains for what we already know. Just be open and let them find you!

# Day 6:

## Embodying the Muse

### AFFIRMATION:

*"I am a muse, a magical creatrix of mythical proportions!"*

In Western mythology, Zeus had nine Divine daughters, each representing various gifts: poetry, music, dance, comedy, art, etc. Today you can be one of them. The archetype of the muse is one of the most delightful embodiments of the Divine Feminine you will ever know. Try it on. Just BE a muse or amusing today and every day. Play music, write poetry and inspire others, whatever turns you on.

I know how much time we all spend trying to "look good." That's not what musing around is about. Now you have permission to be silly. Now, let's get the party started! Get messy with your paints, your pottery or your latest crafty creation. You do not need to take a class because that would require intellect and possibly work. No, we're looking for play mode. It's time to sing in the shower, dance in the rain, jump in the puddles or redecorate!

If you haven't seen the movie, "The Muse" starring Sharon Stone[xxii], it's time to rent it! You'll notice that she inspires others to follow their dreams and believe in magic by merely BEING a muse.

Have you put a creative idea on hold for a while not knowing how to get started? It's time to pull it out of the closet and just go for it. Maybe it's time for a fairy tea party in the garden—don't forget to invite your zany friends. Do you know any other muses? Ask them to play with you. Try to do one thing every day that you've never done before. Learn one new word or song every day. We're looking for novelty here.

My favorite approach to this is how I dress. I love to wear bright colors, unique jewelry and dye my hair various shades of blue. When people see me in public, they light up and curiously ask, "Are you celebrating a special occasion?" I reply, "Yes, I'm a magical moment collector, and I'm collecting magical moments." This invitation usually starts a unique conversation with strangers and lets the universe know what I'm looking for. Lately, I've been collecting self-identified unicorns everywhere. Who knew there were so many unicorns!

My fairy godmother made me a set of cards that work like conversation starters. Have you met your fairy godmother? Well, get one immediately![12] Anyway, the cards are on my breakfast table so that we can get to the juicy questions quickly rather than wasting time with typical small talk.

Your assignment is to be a muse. From this vantage point, what creativity wants to flow? What bubbles up from this empty

---

[12] *You may ask Fifi Fluffinwish for any wish at http://holographicgoddess.com/faerie-godmother-services/. My fairy godmother can be found at http://holographicgoddess.com/about-ariel/ .*

awareness? Will you connect with angels? Will you build a fairy house? Will you hula hoop in the grass or take a photo safari of the flowers around your neighborhood? Sing to them, they like that! Will you send the photos like a secret pen pal to your friends and neighbors just to inspire them with their beauty? Whatever you decide to do, it must bring you joy! "We're not boring God anymore!"

# Day 7:

. . . . . . . . . . . . . . . . .

## Transparency & Vulnerability

## AFFIRMATION:

*"I easily connect with others, especially when I let them see my vulnerability. I am lovable and free to be whom I really am."*

The title of this book is about **freedom**. That's why you are reading it. That's why you are taking these 13 Steps so courageously. What if (while being real under almost any circumstance) you were totally free to be authentically yourself, to share your heart, your imperfections, and your not so "nice" side? Your ticket to freedom is your courage to be transparent.

Being transparent and vulnerable takes effort because our ego desires to keep us safe and NOT to show vulnerability. We are wired to "look good," so it takes a victory of the human spirit to let our guard down and be real. That's why practicing this art in a 13 Step support group or amongst friends strengthens our vulnerability muscles.

Sharing vulnerably is disarming and endearing to those around you.[13] Think about how you feel when a pet lays on its back and shows you its belly. The best part is that showing vulnerability also appears to be contagious. Since everyone is seeking connection and emotional intimacy with others, they just need to feel safe enough to open up to you. If you model this behavior first, those around you may share themselves more fully as well. Think about the generations before us that were more guarded and less likely to say, "I love you" to their children. They are more likely to come around if we keep modeling this behavior.

The purpose of sharing my stories with you throughout this book is to encourage you to do the same. It's incredibly freeing not to have secrets, and to realize that I am not alone or weird in this diverse human family. Self-judgment and shame are the worst prisons I've ever experienced, and I hold the key to both. So, why wouldn't I open my own jail cell? Keeping secrets is different from "privacy" because secrets carry shame or judgment. Secrets are toxic. Privacy, on the other hand, is not emotionally charged. I don't need to share my food journal with you unless I'm judging myself for it.

It's time to explore what stops you from being fully self-expressed. Ask yourself, "What is it that I don't want people to know about me?" Make a list of these fears. Share them, to the extent you can, with as many friends as possible. Allow this sharing to create more intimacy between you and those around you. It will feed you.

Here goes. I fear people will find out that:

---

[13] *Just to be clear, this conversation assumes you are physically safe and want emotional intimacy to connect with the person. This exercise is not recommended when you need to protect yourself from an abusive relationship.*

- ♥ I feel depressed sometimes and anxious underneath my happy façade, especially when I don't exercise or eat well. Until recently, I said, "It's just my thyroid," and avoided my feelings.

- ♥ I fear that I will hurt someone else's feelings by speaking my truth, so I previously held back a lot.

- ♥ I have a lot of gas and constipation often when I don't eat well. It turns out it was SIBO (small intestinal bacterial over-growth).

- ♥ I become cranky sometimes and am not very "nice" to those I love.

- ♥ I used to be better at spending money than saving it.

- ♥ I was sexually curious, as a child. In later years, I felt shame about this. Later, as a workaholic, I was too physically exhausted to be interested in sex most of the time.

A mommy blogger wrote one of the funniest books I ever read. It inspired me to want to share with outrageous honesty. Don't miss *Carry On Warrior*.[xxiii] I also recommend *Outrageous Openness*.[xxiv] Since reading that book, I've begun a sit-down comedy routine to make fun of all things human—from a mermaid's perspective of course. Much of it includes speaking my shame as if it doesn't hook me emotionally anymore.

One more way I express humor in the face of very serious business—I made fun of estate planning, my profession of twenty years, in hopes of inspiring people to get over their fear of writing a will. To see unscripted silliness on the subject, check out my videos. (http://yourlegacylives.com/resources-ask-the-attorney/)

Now it's your turn!

# STEP 7:

........................

## *Fulfillment:*

# YOU CAN HAVE IT ALL

# Day 1:

. . . . . . . . . . . . . . . . .

## Fulfillment

### AFFIRMATION:

*"I awaken each day excited and go to bed each day fulfilled."*

What if you COULD have it all? What would that look like? Is your dream represented on your vision board? If you haven't let yourself have it on your vision board, it's unlikely that you'll let yourself have it in real life.

Once, dressed as a mermaid, I offered a little girl a small gift from my magic bag. She pulled back and said, "No, I have to earn it." This limiting belief will stop her from receiving the fulfillment she may desire unless she works very hard. What prevents you from letting the universe lavish you with everything you desire?

What if you understood how precious you are? What if you understood that in this world, everything is indeed here to support you? When was the last time you asked for fulfillment? At this moment, I grant you permission to "have it all!" Does that help? Try the concept of having it all. What if you settled for more, instead of less?

This is often a radical and audacious way to live. I remember I used to be afraid that if I got everything I desired, others would be jealous and feel resentful toward me until I realized that I also could inspire them to have it all. Why can't we all have it all?

For me, having it all means vibrant health, love, prosperity & lots of joy, but not at the expense of others. I desire abundance such that I can support others to make their dreams come true too (philanthropy). I want clean oceans (no pollution); symbiotic human life with this planet and its creatures (no exploitation); beauty (authentic Self-expression); trust (integrity); peace; adventure; lots of fun and freedom to reach our potential in the arts.

If you met a genie in a bottle, what would you wish for?

# Day 2:

Beauty

## AFFIRMATION:

*"I am beautiful. You are beautiful. Life is beautiful."*

Our essential Self is not our body. Our body is a reflection, like a mirror, of our spirit. When we stand in our spiritual center, our body follows, radiating our true essence, health, and vitality. Bodies do not lie, so when I manifest a health opportunity—aka illness— it is usually a reflection of a spiritual opportunity—a lesson to learn. Once I learned that lesson, I did not need the illness experience any longer.

Our true Self is unique and beautiful. Our body is merely a reflection of our Spirit when no disease is present. Everything I've been taught about what is beautiful often gets in my way, and I now choose to make up my own definition. I've decided that authenticity is beautiful. Courage is beautiful. Novelty is beautiful. Honesty is beautiful. Kindness is beautiful. Poetry, music, architecture, and art are often beautiful. Nourishing food is beautiful. Real beauty bubbles up from the inside.

When I dress in the morning, I listen to what my actual Self-wants to wear. I look for what color, what texture and what jewelry feels like an authentic expression of me. Thinking this way takes the effort to overcome what the media tries to tell me about beauty. Maybe it's time to get real and let go of any clothes that don't feel like the authentic you! If you were a lawyer like me, that might mean letting go of everything in your closet. Perfect. That just makes room for the real you to fill up the closet. Let yourself have it all!

Let your friends know what you're looking for and consider holding a "beauty shower" for your authenticity to emerge. Tell them to dress as their authentic selves and bring you a gift to honor yours. You can even exchange clothes. Maybe you want to let your sexy self-come out to play. What would sexy look like if we expressed it from the inside out rather than from what we think that others find sexy? What would your clothes look like if you could have it all? What would your closet look like? Is there a limiting story about how expensive such a step would be? Let the world know what you're looking for and let it come to you.

For example, when I first began to dress authentically, I couldn't find a store that had crowns, dancing capes, goddess attire, magic wands, mermaid tails and fairy wings—all essentials for me. I decided to open a non-profit store where women could donate or consign such items, and I could resell them. Women loved it and volunteered to work there. It was like playing dress up every day! Eventually, my closet was full of my favorite things, and I sold the store. The next step for me is to have my clothes made as I imagine them to be—using my own designs. If opening a store is not for you and buying a brand-new wardrobe to discover your authenticity is too costly to consider try visiting thrift and consignment stores to begin exploring what your vision looks like.

Don't stop there. Now authentically decorate your bedroom to show who you really are! Next, do your kitchen and continue expanding to your car, the garden, your cubicle at work and the rest of your world until they all are a reflection of the beauty you feel inside of you. Maybe you've always wanted a vegetable garden – buy a plant today, even if it's in a pot. "Ta-da," you have the beginning of your garden!

I like to think of humans as flowers, each uniquely beautiful, with different colors, shapes, sizes, and smells. There is no need for a beauty contest because competition only divides us. Let's enjoy us as one big beautiful, diverse human flower garden instead. Everywhere, may everyone bring our many gifts and talents to the forefront and support each other in being as fully Self-expressed and beautiful as we really are. I realize it may take a victory of the human spirit to overcome our training in competition. Everything is a choice.

Let's talk about size, since being "overweight" is such a big deal in certain parts of the world. In America, our culture currently promotes the idea that large women are not beautiful. In many cultures, it is considered beautiful to be large because of the abundance of food and because not having to work too hard is seen as a good thing. I've heard that here in Hawaii, they used to feed the queen and massage her stomach to be able to eat even more for this reason. Does judging people who are "overweight" serve anyone? Only the weight loss industry benefits from this way of thinking

Consider how some cultures encourage women to be as small as possible. Most of us learned not to let our bodies or possessions take up too much space. We often worry if our nose is too big or our thighs are too wide. For many women, having large breasts brings more attention to our sexuality than most of us might like. That's why so many women prefer to hide their beauty behind their baggy sweatshirts. To be "feminine," we often drive small cars; have small dogs and small purses for evening attire—too small to hold much at all. How have you played small in response to cultural norms? How does it affect your authentic Self-expression today?

Let's assume instead that someone who appears to be "overweight" is actually at the perfect weight for his or her development at this time. Let's believe that our bodies know exactly what we need and not just physically. For example, many years ago while living in Istanbul, I experienced daily sexual harassment and I subconsciously added 30 pounds to my weight. My body was showing me that I needed to learn self-defense. When toxicity is present in my body, I believe I also gain weight to protect my organs from toxins. This is wisdom. What is your weight communicating to you?

# Day 3:

· · · · · · · · · · · · · · · · ·

## Eating for Pleasure

## AFFIRMATION:

*"Food is fun and here for my pleasure. My relationship to food is an exciting adventure!"*

My grandparents were from Montana farmland during the great depression. That meant food was scarce, and they related to it from survival mode. They felt lucky to have food at all and used it for its practical purposes, not for pleasure. I've been living from this place most of my life, except when I use food to numb out my feelings.

In contrast, in a recent movie at a fine restaurant in *Paris Can Wait,* the French person ordered one of everything on the menu just to taste each item. For this person, food was all about pleasure. I've always felt guilty when I enjoyed food for pleasure as if it was something only the wealthy did, and growing up, we weren't that. Allowing myself to order a treat and just have one bite has always felt "wasteful." I'm not suggesting that we go back to the extravagance of Versailles or Rome and eat until we vomit, but I am suggesting that we try on a new way of seeing food. Remember, you are seeking more freedom so that you can choose how to relate to food rather than defaulting to the limiting beliefs passed down to you by your ancestors.

It's time to get curious and try things you've never tried before. It's time to explore and expand. ***Let's have a food adventure!*** I've given up my old drug of choice, sugar. My approach will have that one limitation for the moment, but the rest of the food world is fair game.

It's easy for me to get in a food rut and "not know what to eat." So let's become connoisseurs and not settle for less than the highest quality, organic ingredients, for example, from farmer's markets. Let's take a cooking class, hire a chef, or try new restaurants. Eat avocados every day if that's what's calling you. How many ways can avocado be prepared? If your budget doesn't allow this, get creative.

You now have permission to play with your food—in fact, you must. This is your homework. Try novelty. The presentation is just as important as how it tastes. Use cocktail umbrellas in your smoothies, edible flowers as garnish and beautiful dishes to bring beauty into your life. My favorite thing to do is set the table with crisp linen napkins. I'll never forget when I ordered a cappuccino at a typical café in Amalfi, Italy, and it was served with a silver spoon wrapped in a gold organza bag. Wow!

Do you have a binder or box with all of your favorite recipes? Why not?

I want to see photos of your adventures, and so do other food-ies. Be sure to post some on our Facebook page to inspire the rest of us to play a more beautiful game. *The object of the game is to make food a friend—to make it fun again—rather than feeling like the enemy.* Be as the French when it comes to food—let yourself really enjoy it. It doesn't take a lot of food to satiate our desires when it's enticing and nourishing. If quality food satisfies us, we will stop reaching for the things that deplete us.

Now apply this approach to all things in life (not just food). Fill up your life with the "real thing." Enjoy pleasure and quality relation-ships. Don't settle for less. Try new things to find out what you really love. Life need not feel like you're stuck in a rut. Life is an expansive adventure! Read the books that inspire you. See your favorite mov-ies. Get involved in your community. Jump into your life with both feet. Consider traveling. Be unstoppable. Be the Divine being that you are –let your Goddess out to play! Enjoy—it is why you are here.

# Day 4:

. . . . . . . . . . . . . . . . .

## Become Softer

## AFFIRMATION:

*"As I have the courage to soften, I become even more powerful."*

A woman's sense of safety has a lot to do with weight gain. I taught women's self-defense, and I am a big proponent of learning to fight back. Mahatma Gandhi said, "The mice which find themselves between a cat's teeth acquire no merit from their enforced sacrifice."[xxv] We must have the option to fight back if we are to have real freedom of choice. I've heard that nine out of ten women do not fight back when assaulted, and statistically, fighting back keeps us safer. Since so many women still experience violence, we must learn to be tough.

It makes sense that, in a culture of war or in corporate America, toughness increases the chances of survival. As a lawyer for many years, I know this is true of the culture of our legal system. It's mostly a daily battle of winners and losers. Emotional softness is the last thing I want to embody in such a fight.

Toughness is a defensive reaction that holds us hostage in a culture that chronically presents the conflict as if it's the human norm. Real freedom requires that we have more choices than that. What if we choose to create a culture of cooperation, not one filled with conflict? In some circumstances, wisdom suggests that *softness can be more authentic and therefore stronger than defensiveness.*

If we are soft just to be acceptable as a female in our culture, this is not empowering. *I suggest we practice the art of softness so that it becomes a powerful part of our Divine repertoire* and is readily available when we consciously choose to use it.

"How can I be softer," I ask myself. I could:

- **LET THE WORDS I SPEAK FEEL LIKE HONEY.**

- **CULTIVATE GENTLENESS** with others and me.

- **LISTEN MORE ACTIVELY** to others.

- **LOWER MY EMOTIONAL GUARD** and allow myself to be more vulnerable.

- **BATHE AND MOISTURIZE MY SKIN** releasing hard callouses on my feet.

- **HAVE MORE MASSAGES** to release the wall of muscle that acts as my armor.

- ♥ **STOP JUDGING OTHERS AND MYSELF.**

- ♥ **ALLOW OTHERS TO CONTRIBUTE TO ME** (especially men)

- ♥ **WRITE MORE POETRY.** Read more poetry. Where are all the poets?

- ♥ **HAVE A GOOD CRY.**

Are you wondering how this is stronger than brute force? There is no resistance to gentleness. It's often disarming and softens those around you. Mahatma Gandhi freed all of India from English rule when force could not have prevailed. Martin Luther King's "I have a dream" speech lives on in our hearts, never to be forgotten. Mother Theresa's kindness is a Divine Feminine aspect of humanity –one that makes a powerful difference. I believe that love is the most powerful force in the universe. If you were a gentle warrior and took a different approach to conflict, what would the effect be?

You may be wondering how this practice could possibly relate to food. I ate to protect myself and put on weight as armor. I ate to numb my fears and anxieties when I did not feel safe. I wanted to wear the full burka when I lived in Istanbul to protect myself, and in America, I wear baggy clothes for the same reason. I looked at pictures of "hard" bodies and wanted to be like them. Sometimes, I still hide my softness and hide in a cave like many mermaids. I choose to create a culture of cooperation rather than conflict, where humans will be happier, more authentically self-expressed, and everyone will have enough food to eat.

# Day 5:

## By Invitation Only

### AFFIRMATION:

*"My life is by invitation only. I wisely choose the energies that I allow into my field."*

Your life is by invitation only. You invite whatever shows up in your life. YOU are a magnet for whatever you desire. If you are attracting people who complain all day, congratulations, you have the opportunity to heal that part of you that wants to complain a lot and is triggered by the same patterns in others.

The bad news is that most of our invitations are subconscious. The good news is that we now have a choice. We can consciously invite whatever we desire into our lives. That means we can say "no" whenever we want, and we can say "yes" to our fulfillment. There are more joyful possibilities in my life than I can ever fulfill, so why waste my time on anything less than total joy.

Let's say my desire is for more Self-awareness. I can unconsciously choose a life of suffering to attain this, or I can consciously choose "enlightenment by laughter." That's one of many possibilities. It's my choice if I am awake enough to make it.

Let me bring this down to earth with an example.

I was a wallflower in junior high. I would wait along the wall for someone to ask me to dance, and often no one ever did. Seldom was my desire for connection with the person of my choice fulfilled. Instead, I felt lucky if ANYONE asked me to dance and settled for less than my actual desire. With low self-esteem about "belonging," it never occurred to me that I could:

- ♥ Choose to invite someone that I actually liked to dance.

- ♥ Let someone know that I wanted him/her to ask me to dance.

- ♥ Dance with someone other than the "opposite" sex.

- ♥ Enjoy dancing by myself or in a group.

Without self-esteem, I often held back in life and did not join the dance at all.

Yesterday, I had a breakthrough. For over a year, I have been admiring a free diving group that meets regularly at the beach and supports each other in learning how to hold their breath longer underwater. They are world renown and very serious. Never having taken a freediving class, I felt that I would not be welcome. Coincidentally, I forgot to bring my bathing suit with me for my daily swim.

Determined to swim anyway, I decided to wear my beautiful flowing dress over my mermaid tail and even left my extravagant shell necklace on. I looked like I was going to an underwater ball in all the fabric! This was perfect attire for my first official free dive introduction, Ha, Ha.

I swam out to meet these free divers who were from all over the world. One could hold her breath for 8 minutes and dive down to 68 meters (over 200 feet). My attire amused them, and they invited me to see how deep I could go for my first time. I was so excited that it didn't matter that I was decked out in a mermaid ball gown and had no training, no weights, nor equipment other than my mermaid fin. I dove 10 meters easily, enjoyed the ride, and I will definitely return to play again with my new friends. They gave me tips and ideas on how to improve my technique. The moral of the story is to "get over it" and jump in! Hint—Sometimes it helps to do something crazy to get out of your ego.

Where do you hold back for fear of rejection? Where do you judge yourself? What would you do if you were fearless? How can you be an invitation to others? How can you assume they are just as afraid as you are to ask for a dance? You can either let them know that you're open to their invite, or you can choose to take the lead. This is a metaphor for everything!

So what if our worst fear occurs. So what if we are rejected the first time. It means nothing unless I make up a deflating story about it. I'm good at making up stories, so now I choose only to invite empowering stories into my life. A typical rejection story can become a story of being unstoppable—where I continue to ask for what I want in creative ways until I attain it. My new story is about my demonstrated commitment to never take "no" for an answer when it comes to my dreams. I am unstoppable if I choose to be.

My experience of fulfillment may have nothing to do with external circumstances, but if I decide to manifest something, an invitation of the act or word primes the pump.

# Day 6:

## Have A Love Affair with Everything!

### AFFIRMATION:

*"I am a love magnet! I am here to have a love affair with everything!"*

How can I love more deeply, unconditionally and without limitation? In the past, I thought I could only have a love affair with "Mr. Right." I was so wrong!

Love is so much more than romance or sexual intercourse! I'm talking about choosing to love someone or something the way it wants to be loved and the way I want to love it, which may or may not include any physical connection. There's an energetic exchange with every person, creature or rock we meet during this lifetime.

For example, I communed with a *flower* one day in the garden. I asked how *it* wanted to be loved, and I listened intensely. It shared stories and wisdom beyond anything I had imagined. I was inspired to write a children's book during that conversation. I genuinely love this flower now whenever I see it.

I've opened my heart to *eating an orange* and really appreciating how delicious it tasted. I had taken them for granted before. They seemed boring by themselves. Eating an orange, I discovered, can be ecstatic when I actually stop mindfully to taste it uninterrupted.

Have you ever made love to *the moon?* Take a bath in the rays of the moon and see what unfolds.

I love *water* more than anything else. There's just nothing quite like a long hot shower or a candlelight bath.

I have a love affair with *the ocean* every morning in Hawai'i. It's such a beautiful place to be one with nature. What an extraordinary array of life forms in every color, size, and shape. I've never experienced more diversity than a coral reef. It lights me up, and I show love to it by picking up any garbage I find. I raise funds to clean up the ocean whenever I can. They don't call us "merMAIDS" for nothing.

Who says love affairs can't be entirely innocent. You probably love your family and your pets and even your friends already! Now, expand that circle. It's natural to love everything because that is our essence. Let it flow. We all crave connection and emotional intimacy. We can have love with or without acts of sexuality. It's your choice.

In the world of romance, I love my spouse, and I choose monogamy because the focus on one relationship allows me to focus more intensely. It also enables me to devote more time to exploring and loving the universe around me.

Why limit myself when I can adore the beauty I see in everyone and everything? Since I trust myself not to have sex with everyone I find attractive, it's safe to let myself FEEL sexy most of the time. It's not healthy to turn off our natural chemistry, and I choose not to allow chemistry control my behavior. Instead, I choose to focus that energy on my creative projects. That's how this book happened! Because I AM a love magnet that knows that, I am capable of having a love affair with anything. Right now, I'm having a love affair with this book as I write it, as I let it into my life, and as I edit it repeatedly.

How would your life be different if you let yourself have a love affair with everything?

Start with something easy, such as some part of your body you genuinely admire. Have you taken the time to have a love affair with your own body lately? Does it feel loved? Does it feel appreciated? What does it want? Have you stopped to listen?

Now move on to the more challenging fun. Try loving something that you wouldn't usually love, like a stranger. Try waiters for example. Whenever you go to a restaurant, fall in love with your server. Let the server know how much you appreciate their service. Find out something about the server that you didn't know before. Tip the server well. You can just adore this person without having to take it any further—you don't have to sleep with the server.

Now consider something even harder. Maybe you're getting a speeding ticket from a policeman. How can you love the officer more deeply even at that moment? What if you complimented the officer's professionalism and said how much you appreciated how safe you feel having him or her in your community?

Once you remember how easy it is to love yourself and everything that you come into contact with, you'll realize that the entire universe loves you that much too! You consist of atoms that are held together by magnetism which create an energy around your body. You project your feelings to others through this energy. *When you love yourself and everything around, you are one big love magnet.* Don't get in the way! Light yourself up! Be sure to share the intimate details with your support circle so they can fall in love with you more too.

When I am a love magnet and allow myself to love and be loved, I reach for food less.

# Day 7:

## I Don't React, I Respond

## AFFIRMATION:

*"I am not my emotional reactions. I choose to respond from love instead."*

A great person once said that I could find my purpose in life by answering three questions:

1. What's the problem?

2. What's the need?

3. How can I help?

The design of this inquiry helped me understand that I often feel fulfilled by fixing problems for others. If I correctly identify the problem, this approach can work for a while. Helping others is why I was a lawyer for twenty years, but I ended up feeling resentful and overwhelmed because I took on too much responsibility to "fix" their problems. However, this approach really is just a Band-Aid because the three questions were born from a limited paradigm. The questions assume that (1) There *is* a problem, (2) *I* need to fix it, and (3) My value lies only in what I can contribute to others. This old paradigm is reactionary and comes from a place that "something is wrong" requiring it to be fixed. Let's raise the bar!

Now, hang with me for a moment. Let's begin our inquiry instead from "there's nothing wrong, and there's nothing to fix." Let's assume that everything and everyone are perfect right now, in a spiritual sense, and exactly where they need to be on their journey. That means, the world doesn't "need" me, and there's no one to convert to my way of thinking. Ouch! That means I don't have a corner on what's real or what's right. Yikes! Now, what shall I do with this one wild and precious life? Can you feel your ego freaking out yet? If indeed, the world doesn't need me, then life doesn't mean anything, and that it doesn't mean anything that it doesn't mean anything.[14] Try that on! Do you feel your resistance to the idea that your life is meaningless?

Humans resist this possibility because we are meaning-creating machines. We're wired to make meaning of everything. I hope that I think of some worthy sense of things and that I do so on purpose, not by default!

Let's revisit the three-question inquiry from this new paradigm. Since there is nothing to react to, I can choose to respond instead. Let's read that again, "Since there is nothing to react to, I can choose to respond instead."

---

[14] *A saying from Landmark Education. (landmarkworldwide.com)*

Being reactionary is helpful if I'm in a cave with a tiger. Reacting could save my life. Reacting to everything in my life would be a constant nightmare given how circumstances change regularly, but this is how most of us live our lives.

*Responding,* on the other hand, provides clarity and freedom to choose. It is a much more powerful place to stand. Most of us have learned the wisdom of "cooling down" a bit before addressing something that upsets us—if we want our relationship to last long term. After we come out of our reactionary mode, we have more clarity of mind to respond instead. Here's one of my favorite examples:

> *There was a Zen Master who was very pure, very illumined. Near the place where he lived there happened to be a food store. The owner of the food store had an unmarried daughter. One day she was found with child. Her parents flew into a rage. They wanted to know the father, but she would not give them the name. After repeated scolding and harassment, she gave up and told them it was the Zen Master. The parents believed her. When the child was born, they ran to the Zen Master, scolding him with a foul tongue, and they left the infant with him. The Zen Master said, "Is that so." This was his only comment.*xxvi

> *He accepted the child. He started nourishing and taking care of the child. By this time, his reputation had come to an end, and he was an object of mockery. Days ran into weeks, weeks into months and months into years. But, there is something called conscience in our human life, and the young girl was tortured by her conscience. One day she finally disclosed*

*to her parents the name of the child's real father, a man who worked in a fish market. The parents again flew into a rage. At the same time, sorrow and humiliation tortured the household. They came running to the spiritual Master, begged his pardon, narrated the whole story and then took the child back.*

*His only comment was "Is that so."[xxiii]*

This story shows us that we can make various choices instead of choosing to react. Whether the Zen master made the "right" choice or not isn't what matters to me. What is important to me is the *freedom to choose.* It's impossible to respond from love or emotional intelligence when I simply react to circumstances. Had I been the Zen master, I would not have seen another approach, because I would have been so preoccupied with the injustice of the accusation. If I'm reacting all the time, I never choose how my life will go; I'm allowing myself to be tossed about by my apparent circumstances.

How do I get out of reactionary mode when an emotional crisis triggers me? I modified what the firefighter taught me to do as a child: "stop, drop & roll." Now I *"stop, drop & love!"* I stop my reactionary internal monologue long enough to drop my old story that isn't working (i.e., there's something wrong), and I choose to respond from love instead. Love is alive and well inside of all of us. Outside of reactionary judgment, we can always remember our unconditional love because that is the essence of who we really are. I hope that my life is remembered as that of the Zen master—as an example of how to choose freely regardless of the circumstances.

Perhaps the more compelling questions to answer are:

1. What is working?

2. How can I be more authentically Self expressed?

3. How can my small self (ego) move out of the way?

# STEP 8:

. . . . . . . . . . . . . . . . .

# Rediscover Your Passion

# Day 1:

. . . . . . . . . . . . . . . .

## What is your Passion?

### AFFIRMATION:

*"I am on fire with passion burning clear and brilliant."*

What makes you swing your tail out of bed in the morning? What are you passionate about? What would you do for a living if you didn't have to worry about money, family or about what other people might think?

Being a mermaid inspires me, but few people understand what that means to me. I woke up this morning determined to translate my mermaid passion into plain English so that I could share it with you. Here it goes,

> *"Mermaids **inspire** us to share our **gifts, wisdom,** and **beauty,** and to fall in love with the **oceans** again."*

I can best describe my five passions using this description of mermaids:

1. I wish to **INSPIRE** others with a passion. I'm a muse and thoroughly enjoy watching others light up with joy, laughter, and insight. As a mermaid "sit down" comedian with a terrible memory for details or punchlines, I often have the opportunity to witness these moments.

2. I love passionately to bring out the **GIFTS** and talents that each of us uniquely carries. When you are stuck in a boring job, you need to pay the rent, and you are numbed out by eating ice cream in front of the TV, it's easy to lose sight of your greatest talents. I enter my garden of delight when I watch others bloom into their joy and freedom.

3. I have a passion for **WISDOM**. I love to collect quotes, stories, and metaphor as if I'm on a spiritual adventure. I feel expanded when I discover the truth at a deeper level than ever before. It's like unlocking a secret garden door.

4. I have an uncontrollable passion for **BEAUTY**—it just explodes wherever I go. It mesmerizes me; I feel its Divine origins and desire communion with it. My definition of beauty is "How authentic is its expression?"

5. I have a passion for the **OCEANS**. There is no place I'd rather be, assuming they're clean. The mostly unexplored ocean is a vast playground. I make friends with new creatures almost every day.

If you're not sure where to start to discover your passion, here are some ideas:

- ♥ Use the vision board exercise discussed previously to see images that inspire you. This can help tremendously. If you prefer computers, phones or tablets for viewing images, use Pinterest to find inspiring images for example.

- ♥ Turn on your favorite music to get your juices flowing and dance around the house for a while. I just Googled "inspirational songs," and I immediately found 42 of them. Once I find a song I like, I used Pandora to find more.

- ♥ Ask your friends and family where they think your passions lie. Say, "Hey mom, what do you think is my greatest passion in life?"

- ♥ Remember a time, such as your childhood, when you had a dream to be or do something extraordinary. There is usually a clue about your passions in these memories.

- ♥ Look at your hobbies. When you travel or take a vacation, what activities appeal to you?

- ♥ Decide what your favorite books and movies are. There is usually a theme, to find it begin to connect the dots without judgment, like a six-year-old getting ready for the show and tell.

- ♥ Find the themes of your favorite conversations. Most people want to discuss things that light them up. Perhaps you would like to speak about your passions—animals, children, chocolate, space exploration, math, relationships, or whatever they may be. You'll notice that you "light up" when you discuss your passions. If it doesn't light you up, then it's not your thing.

You are free to follow your passions or not, as you choose. I ask that you at least know what they are, and begin to share your passion statement with those you trust. A passion statement is short, precise, and inspires you just in speaking it. Say it to yourself as often as you can.

The more you share it with others, the more real it will become, and then when you forget why you're here, others will begin to remind you. When I went to a coffee shop the other day, a woman I had not met before said, "Oh, you're that mermaid. You're funny!" I thought, "Oh yeah! That's me." The magic has begun.

# Day 2:

· · · · · · · · · · · · · · · · ·

## A Life of Wonder!

## AFFIRMATION:

*"Life is an adventure and full of surprises. I am curious to experience the world with fresh eyes and an open heart."*

Remember when you were a child and everything seemed new and you were eager to learn? That was a state of wonder. Do you remember your first snowfall—your first ice cream—your first kiss? The beginner's mind of wonder is quickly lost as we age and, often, we become "know-it-alls" or cynics. To feel wonder is to bask in the mystery of it all. Did you ever find out why the moon looks so much larger on the horizon than it looks directly above you? When did you stop asking "Why?"

What if your life could be WONDERful again—like the world you experienced as a child when you experienced things for the first time? What if to have this life all it took was a decision to approach life from a place of wonderment? What if you decided that, when viewed with fresh eyes and an open heart, EVERYTHING could be WONDERful. What would you ask? What would you do? How would you feel?

When was the last time you went to an art museum? What takes your breath away? When did you last dance in the rain? Have you made it to Paris yet? If not Paris, then where is your dream destination? Anything is possible!

Is it possible that just under the surface there are great aspects of your *family* that you haven't discovered yet? When was the last time you had a real, emotionally intimate conversation with those you love? What if you approached them with curiosity and without any assumptions or judgment as if this was the first time you met them?

Have you ever taken an *inner adventure* during meditation? Allowing your inner vision to transport you like a magic carpet ride wherever your heart wants to go is a journey into the unknown. If you haven't enjoyed your inner landscape lately, then it's time to take a test drive. What are you driving nowadays?

Now, let's step into *your closet*, as you've never seen your clothes before. Pretend they're not even yours and you have no attachment. What do you like? What drags you down? Is it messy? Is it inspiring? Is it like a treasure hunt? What if your wardrobe were magical? Is it time to give something away? Is it time to reinvent something? Don't allow practicality or the price you paid for something limits your responses. How can this wardrobe support your authentic Self-expression – the very reason you are here on this planet? You have permission to start over completely. You are not the same person that you were when you collected these items.

So what are you waiting for? Why are you still reading when you could be in awe and wonder of our world today – a world that you've never seen before? It's a new day. Be curious!

What does WONDER mean to you?[15]

---

[15] *Check out www.LiveInWonder.com by Eric Saperston.*

# Day 3:

. . . . . . . . . . . . . . . . .

## Freedom

## AFFIRMATION:

*"I am free. I have always been free. I will always be free. I decide how my life goes."*

Like so many people, I created my own golden cage, by buying into the idea that I had to HAVE a college education, to HAVE a good job, to HAVE money, all *so I could be free* to DO or BE whatever I wanted. Forty years later, I discovered that I was less open to DO or BE whatever I wanted because I owed so much debt from financing my future freedom. After paying off the debt, I wasn't free either, because now I was supposed to own a house and save for retirement *so I could be free* to do whatever I wanted later in life. That's actually backward. The truth is, if I AM who it is that I want to be NOW (freedom), and take steps to DO what is necessary to have what I want (freedom), then I will HAVE it. I decide how my life goes, but first I have to break free from limited thinking.

True freedom is mine from birth, even if I'm born into oppression. There is always a choice if I am careful not to give this power away. I could choose to live and travel nomadically with few possessions and no place to call "home" like many gypsies. Mermaids have even more freedom from traditional roles and consumer culture. They don't have to work or pay rent. Only humans made up that game and attached meaning to owning land. The ocean doesn't make it easy to create artificial boundaries that separate us from each other.

What freedom have you been longing for? Is it time to have the relationship of your dreams? Do you yearn to travel? Do you want to make a movie? What is holding you back?

Most of the people I meet have decided that their responsibilities to their family keep them from being free. I believe that's just an excuse. I don't think it's tough to enroll your family into your dreams. If you said, "Honey, I have a dream of going to a little island in the South Pacific one day, renting a sailboat and spending a summer exploring the ocean." Don't you think your family would want to join you or at least enjoy making that happen for you? The universe wants to make our dreams come true, and your family and friends want to do so even more. The only thing that gets in the way is fear created by limiting beliefs. So, let's talk about freedom from limiting beliefs.

How we see things is just our perception—it's not "real." We see things through our mental lens, most of which is based on a past experience and habitual thinking. The only way out of this illusion is to break free of how we have thought about something in the past and create a new neural pathway. If we want new thoughts, we have to invite them in, or we will by default just get more of the past. Affirmations, Neuro-linguistic programming, hypnosis, visualization and Emotional Freedom Technique (EFT) are great ways to create new neural pathways. It's like brainwashing ourselves to have beliefs that actually serve us rather than just accepting our previous brainwashing—the thoughts that tear us down.

Imagine actually choosing your own belief system instead of just inheriting someone else's dysfunction. This could create a radical shift in how you perceive reality, which in turn may create new behaviors (particularly around food and addiction).

What are you waiting for?

# Day 4:

· · · · · · · · · · · · · · ·

## Down to Earth in my Body

## AFFIRMATION:

*"I am the soul that lives in this body-temple. I love my body. I honor my body. I am so grateful and happy to care for my body."*

Many women I've met seem to hover somewhere above their bodies and, for whatever reason, don't relate much to the physical aspects of being on this planet. Like them, sometimes it takes a massage or vigorous exercise to remind me that I have a body at all.

Addictive behaviors are not just spiritual in nature, but also physically motived. After so many years of poor eating habits and chemical reactions to particular foods, it feels like I have an allergy to sugar. I eat it, and my body craves more. Recognizing the physical craving cycle is essential. For that, we can apply some concrete strategies that can get us out of the addictive cycle in the first place or build a stronger bridge to help maintain abstinence in the future:

1. Walnuts

   Our brain is shaped like these amazing nuts for some reason. They magically stabilize my blood sugar and minimize my cravings. Have them on hand to support your nutrition program.

2. Gymnema

   This magical supplement changes my taste buds and makes sweet taste bitter. I tried each dessert today, and it tasted terrible as if someone made a serious baking error!

3. Buddy System

   Always have a buddy you can call before you reach for the sugar and break your sobriety. That's what buddies are for! You can also ask for help from friends, family, angels, elementals and your higher power when you need it! Join a support group as part of your recovery.

4. Exercise

   I'm much less likely to eat sugar when am I am exercising. Just go for a walk instead and change your body chemistry with endorphins for the moment.

5. Naps

   I may just be reaching for food because I'm tired, I'll give myself a healthy treat and take a nap. Nappers are said to live longer.

## 6. Alternatives

Have lots of fun, healthy alternatives in your possession. That means your pantry, your car, and your purse. One of my favorites is a blueberry right out of the freezer. I recently tried frozen bananas through a Champion juicer. It tasted just like ice cream. Then I added some chopped macadamia nuts on top for a crunchy sundae.

## 7. Treats for yourself

Another alternative is to create a deck of cards. Each one has a treat on it. It may say, "Candlelight Bath," or "Get a Massage" or "Watch a Good Movie" or "Ask Your Sweetie to Cuddle." Choose a card whenever you want a treat. Make a list of the non-food treats you love and post them on the refrigerator. See my list attached as Exhibit F.

## 8. Nutrition Plans

Of course, having great meals all day long is the best prevention. Put this in place, and you won't have to worry too much. This is the hardest part for me because I'm not yet in the habit and after I get a plan in place, I feel like my own program is trying to control me. The little three-year-old inside of me wants to rebel immediately. I realize this sounds crazy, but most of our stories are. Keeping a food journal helps me tremendously. I strongly recommend it, especially if the idea makes you cringe.

## 9. Connections with Loved Ones.

Emotional intimacy may be what you're ***really*** wanting.

Let yourself have it. Make it happen and ask for 100% of what you desire. Trust that others wish to contribute to you and it is their job to say, "Yes" or "No" authentically to your requests.

# Day 5:

· · · · · · · · · · · · · · · · ·

## Embracing Ecstasy

## AFFIRMATION:

*"I am a fountain of ecstasy flowing to others!"*

If our true nature is joy and love, then all we have to do is determine what is in the way of our ecstatic experience and invite it to get out of the way. In my case, I carried a lot of sexual shame and guilt as a child, and it followed me into adulthood, getting in the way of the ecstasy of intimacy. If you let yourself have joy in your life, what would it look like? What gets in the way of your ecstasy?

I imagine myself like a fountain of youth, with waters of life flowing endlessly and abundantly through me. I let this etheric water flow energetically around me and through me with the intention of renewal at all times. It acts as a force field of love, continually replenishing itself and it does not allow foreign energy into my flow except by conscious invitation. I believe that disease has no place in this fountain of joy. I don't need sickness or pain as an excuse to leave my body when my work here is complete. My soul will release when the time comes in ecstatic bliss, regardless of how the circumstances may appear.

Do you like to dance the tango? Would it help if you took a Tantra class? How about pole dancing? Have you always wanted to decorate your bedroom with faux fur leopard prints? Do you own a silky robe or pajamas? How do you like to get in touch with your ecstatic bliss? Do you have a sexy music playlist? When was the last time you had a candlelight bath with essential oil and rose petals? If you are not sure, then you're not alone. Your homework is to get your groove on. The test of your success is whether you end up saying, "Yummy!"

# Day 6:

. . . . . . . . . . . . . . .

## Don't Ask Permission to Go "Wild"

## AFFIRMATION:

*"I play my own game and write my own rules. I don't need to ask anyone's permission to be me. I am bold and audacious when I choose to be."*

Whether you are a man or a woman, the wild Divine Feminine is inside you! We all carry our ancestors' genes and DNA memory. If salmon can find their way back to their ancestral river one-hundred years after the dam is removed, so can we! Indigenous wisdom and instinct are here to serve us when we remember how to tap into them.

I am not talking about going wild like a rebellious reaction against something we don't like. I'm talking about a conscious choice not to follow cultural norms but to follow our more primal directives. I like the saying, "Well-behaved women seldom make history."[xxvii]

So, if you were to stop and listen to your primal instincts, what would they say? In the past, I used to judge the primal part of me as not "nice" and not "refined." I was trained to be a "good girl" and feel superior to those who didn't "tow the line" or follow the rules. It still takes effort for me to access this wild part of myself. This is the part of me that isn't afraid to hunt for my meal, have a pet snake, go hiking in the mountains, paint my body with mud clay at the dead sea, shake a rattle, be a shaman, and dance around a campfire with friends. It's time to build your fire, both physically and metaphorically. It's time to stop apologizing all the time if that's a pattern for you. It's time to give yourself a permission slip to play hooky for once. Have you always wanted jaguar print heels and a faux fur coat? True freedom means that you have all options open to you – the freedom to be real even when it's not "nice."

You might wonder, "But what if people think I'm going through a mid-life crisis?"

What we consider a mid-life crisis may just be a reaction to something that feels so stifling that it causes someone to dramatically rebel to access his or her authenticity. However, it may be a very empowering event to finally taking power back from a cultural norm. It doesn't usually work well, however, for the closest family members who may have relied on their old way of being. New freedom may feel like a betrayal to the community because they have become accustomed to and dependent on the old way of being. We, of course, are responsible for creating that dependency and should act responsibly in stopping it by empowering others. By empowering others, we regain our freedom and decide to fulfill our dreams. It doesn't need to be a rebellion. It can be mutually supportive.

**We can ALL have it ALL!**

My fairy godmother just called, and she has granted each of us our freedom. It's time to discover what freedom looks like for you. What will you do TODAY with this one wild and precious life?

# Day 7:

· · · · · · · · · · · · · · · · · ·

## Choosing Vitality

## AFFIRMATION:

*"I choose Vitality!"*

Vitality, like happiness, is simply a result of making empowering choices around what we use to fuel our body, mind, and spirit. We must choose it repeatedly as we do our lives. We can use quality food as fuel, or less-than-whole foods can deplete us. That's because processed and overcooked foods usually don't have what we need to digest the food, so our bodies deplete our stores of these missing components to process them.

Similarly, we can participate in relationships that inspire, or they can drain us. We can exercise in ways that invigorate us, or it can injure us. We can say, "I'm exhausted" all the time and wonder why we feel that way. We can eat sugar and wonder why we feel like we're riding an emotional roller coaster. We can drink too much and wonder why we have a hangover. Each choice we make today either contributes to our vitality or takes away from it, it either creates healthy habits or is a withdrawal from our well-being bank account.

Let's imagine we're using puzzle pieces to build a bridge for ourselves from the old ways of being to the new habits that we desire. Each little piece of the puzzle we lay each day makes the bridge stronger and supports us into the future. In my bridge, I choose to add the following practical puzzle pieces:

- ♥ **Daily exercise**. I like exercise that burns fat rather than muscle by keeping me mostly in my parasympathetic nervous system rather than the sympathetic, i.e., in an anaerobic state. That means I prefer circuit training that doesn't do an exercise for more than 8 seconds. I rest in between each repetition. I do not aspire to the "No pain, no gain" school of thought. I prefer to think of my exercise as a "body meditation." Restorative yoga is also excellent for me because it focuses on the breath and feels like I've had a massage by the time I'm done. This feels like a more Feminine approach than "boot camp" or competitive sports of my childhood. I enjoy the aerobic activity, such as swimming or dancing— just for fun—but not to stress me. Mermaids don't like stress and are never in a hurry.

- ♥ **DAILY MEDITATION**. Dropping into my center to remember who I really am is key to how my life goes. Otherwise, spiritual amnesia sets in. I easily access my essential Self when I empty myself and simply BE. I listen for guidance. I listen for inspiration. I listen for the joy that bubbles up, for the tears that want to come, and for the love that is in my heart. I need from five to fifty minutes for this every day

♥ **AFFIRMATIONS**. I like to read my purpose statement and affirmation(s) each morning (See Exhibit E).

> ♡ *"I am a fountain of love and beauty on an adventure to remember our Divine gifts."*

> ♡ Feel free to use my affirmations as a starting point, but add your own and customize them for yourself.

♥ **VISUALIZATION**. I look at my vision board, imagine that it is already true, and take a moment to feel the fantastic feelings that follow.

♥ **GRATITUDE**. My life is so blessed that I say "thank you" to my higher power for all of its support. I love to share my gratitude with others throughout the day as well. This attitude attracts even more blessings.

♥ **FOOD**. I choose the most nourishing and healthiest food and prepare it with love so that my food plan supports my life purpose and vitality.

♥ **WILLINGNESS TO ASK FOR HELP.** Since the universe is conspiring to surprise and delight me, it is critical that I remain open to receiving these gifts. I must invite help in and gracefully accept it. I always try to have at least one coach who will hold me accountable and keep me moving in the direction of my dreams. A support group is also a key component of success in the express lane to transformation. My vitality support team consists of my spouse, my naturopathic doctor, my massage therapist, my colon hydro-therapist, my life coaches, those who are more etheric–family who have passed on, angels, fairies. Sometimes I add aquatic body-work, essential oils, acupuncture, cranial osteopathy, and classical homeopathy to get energy moving.

- ♥ **WISDOM READINGS**. I love to read inspirational books, quotes, poetry, and sacred texts. I am a sponge for knowledge especially when it opens my heart.

- ♥ **INTEGRITY**. My life only goes as well as my relationships. To be in integrity with others and myself, means being honest and acting in alignment with my true Self. I continually restore or fall out of integrity with the words I use and the actions I take. Being true to my word creates trust and prosperity. My vitality exists in direct proportion to my commitment to integrity.

- ♥ **MUSIC**. I like to sing as much as possible, especially songs that uplift me like my theme song. I love to play music that improves my mood. For example, listen to "You Raise Me Up" sung by Josh Grobin[xxviii].

- ♥ **HUMOR**. I love to laugh. One of my greatest joys is to make others laugh, especially about the human condition.

- ♥ **CONTRIBUTION**. It feels good to contribute to others. I love to make a difference in the lives of others and leave each place better than I found it. This helps me remember that

I am not the center of the universe. One of my passions is cleaning the oceans—one beach at a time.[16]

What are the puzzle pieces you are using to build your bridge to vitality?

---

[16] *I contribute to organizations that support cleaning up and conserving our oceans such as All One Ocean, which is a project of the Earth Island Institute, they can be found at www.AllOneOcean.com.*

# STEP 9:

........................

## *Reclaim Your Power*

# Day 1:

## You are Powerful

### AFFIRMATION:

*"I am powerful to create each day of my life deliberately. I choose to stand in my power. Why? Because I say so."*

This is where the rubber meets the road! It's time to identify where we give our power away and reclaim it. In the 12 Step program, for example, the mantra was, "I am powerless over food." Why would I choose to give my power away to food? Say instead, "*I* am the one in charge of food. *I* decide what does or does not go into my mouth!" This is a declaration of power.

However, it isn't about exercising your personal willpower to dominate your addictive habits. That's just your small ego trying to maintain control by restrictive dieting. That's been shown not to work, or you wouldn't be reading this book! This declaration is bigger than that. It is said by your BIG mythic Self that commands how your life goes, and for whom the entire universe conspires in support just to play along with the game you're making up at this moment. Take time to feel the difference. Our world has been ruled by domination and sees lack of willpower as weakness. Rarely are we trained in the type of power that does not seek to dominate or control. This type **stands in our truth regardless of the circumstances but does not need to dominate** others in the process.

This mythic power is generated not from fear, but *from love* and holds an underlying trust that all is well. It is like a mother who stands solidly for the greatness of her children but does not try to control what they ultimately become. It is like supporting a butterfly with an open hand knowing that its nature is to fly away. In our immaturity, we sometimes hold the butterfly too tightly hoping it will stay and then not understanding why it feels trapped. Do you know any marriages like this?

To identify where we give our power away, ask yourself, *"Where have I become resigned and cynical?"* Is it about your weight? Money? Politics? Religion? Technology? The news? Is it a relationship where you have given up hope? A dream you have given up on happening? Is it a conversation that you always avoid? **Make a list.**

Chronic yeast infections are what I am resigned to. For over 20 years, it feels like I'm fighting a low-grade infection which continues to rob me of energy I'd rather spend somewhere else. Now I think my immune system is even resigned about it. In the past, I have tried and failed to follow the strict dietary guidelines suggested to starve the yeast. In the past, I wasn't able to give up the sugar.

*Now ask yourself what your payoff is for giving away power.* In my case, I didn't have to be responsible for what I decided to eat because I was an "addict." I wanted to eat whatever I wanted whenever I wanted. I didn't have to take the time or energy to plan meals. I could simply revert to my comfort foods and numb out. My rebel said, "You can't tell me what to eat!"

*Now ask yourself what price you pay.* This is the most important question and requires that you really get in touch with the cost to you. I struggled daily with feeling like I'm in a mental fog. I wanted to take a nap and didn't have the energy to do the things I loved to do. Sometimes I was so physically uncomfortable that I couldn't function at all and lived in the bathtub. I was irritable. I felt isolated and ashamed. I didn't feel sexy. I felt sad and hopeless.

*Are you willing to have a breakthrough?* I've read that Jesus never healed anyone without first asking him or her if he or she wanted to be healed. That was no mistake. Miracles don't happen until we're ready. Are you ready?

If you answered, "Yes," then it is time for you to take your power back from the circumstances, as you perceive them. You do so by replacing the old story with a new one. For example, the new story might be, "I'm the possibility of power and freedom in all aspects of my life." Pick an affirmation that inspires you!

When old tapes of despair are playing like mine was this morning, "I can't believe you're at Step #9 and you are still showing symptoms of sugar addiction! You should be over it by now!" In the face of eating two cinnamon rolls today, I can honestly say, "I AM the possibility of love and forgiveness, of fresh starts and LOTS OF FUN!" I'm free to not judge myself and not make it mean anything. I'm free to create my life new at each moment. I'm courageous to be vulnerable and share this deeply personal conversation with the world. I'm powerful to make a new choice, not from a reaction, but from my stand – my stand for vitality! *When I'm in a funk, I just reach for a new story, which generates a better feeling, and take my power back!* I'm free to recommit to building my bridge to vitality at each moment.

I know at first it sounds too simple to just declare a new reality, generate a new feeling and "take my power back." It's kind of like waving a magic wand. It actually does work, especially if you let go of how you think it should unfold. For example, the healing process often gets worse before it gets better. When we clean our closets, the same is true. We pull everything out of the closet before we neatly put it all back in. Cleaning up our lives isn't always "pretty." However, cleaning up our lives can be the most beautiful thing we ever do.

If this is a new muscle for you, expect it to take some practice. You didn't expect to train for a marathon in one day, and so new muscles take some time to strengthen. Just begin to make these declarations for all the areas in your life where you have felt resigned or cynical. Let the universe figure out the "how" is that possible part. When you feel moved to take an action step, do so. Don't force it, and you don't have to do it all. Remember the universe is conspiring with you.

Make your intention known, let the universe know you're committed, and let the rest unfold with grace and ease.

# Day 2:

There are no victims here!

## AFFIRMATION:

*"I choose my life. I choose my story. I choose it all."*

There's a common denominator to a very disempowering story, which we hear more often than we care to admit. It's the story that we are somehow victims of circumstance. I'm not interested in discussing whether it's true or not. That's a conversation for intellects and egos. I'm only interested in whether the victim story is a powerful place to stand and whether we might want to consider another story.

We've all known someone who goes through life as a perpetual victim, and like a self-fulfilling prophecy keeps recreating the same miserable scenarios repeatedly but with different people. This isn't a coincidence and isn't usually done consciously. It's just seen as bad luck like an old country song where a lover cheats on someone and then his or her dog dies. Do you know someone whose life has become like an old country song? They might be the most wonderful person in their heart, but it's hard to be around them when they sound like a broken record.

Have you ever met someone who was just the opposite—someone who always seems to win at everything? Maybe it's a bully who just inherited a lot of wealth, and everything appears to fall into their lap. This is the kind of person who even when they fail at something, rewrites the story to say they hit a home run instead. Doesn't it seem unfair that the universe would reward such a liar? I expose both extremes (the victim and the bully) so that I can remember that the universe doesn't reward us for being a good or a bad person. *The universe is merely conspiring with whatever story we tell.*

The victim story is one of the most repeated and prevalent stories in our culture. It is rewarded with sympathy from others and allows us to avoid any responsibility. Nice! The problem is that it creates a vortex of victimhood. The more we tell our victim stories, the more we create ourselves as a victim, and the universe responds accordingly.

What happened just happened. If we like what happened, then let's focus on it and retell *that* story! If we don't like what happened, then let's learn quickly what didn't work about it and move on to focus on what *does* work in our lives.

You could instead declare yourself victorious! You don't have to be a victim anymore! That old story doesn't serve you. Let it go.

If you're resisting these suggestions, then it may help to look at whether you have so identified with the story that your identity is being challenged. For example, my girlfriend was diagnosed with breast cancer a couple of years ago. The nurse told her that she was now "someone with breast cancer" and could be a model for Friday's fashion show to raise money for cancer research. She was suddenly part of a special club of pink-ribboned women whose identity was all about becoming a "cancer survivor." Either way, the focus was on cancer.

The danger is that the more we concentrate on cancer and identify with it, the more we magnetize the energy of it. I'm not suggesting that we pretend we don't have cancer, but I AM suggesting that it may be a more powerful stand to say, "I am a healthy, happy, radiant woman!" If we are longing for a sense of belonging, we might want to join a club that promotes vitality rather than one that focuses on the perceived problem.

Once we let an old victim story go, we must replace it immediately with something more powerful. Otherwise, inertia will fill the vacuum without any new input (more of the old). My friend could have told herself an empowering story about the same circumstances. For example, "I chose to have a cancer experience so I could discover things about myself I never knew before. I found out just how lovable I really am, I found my courage, I allowed others to contribute to me, I realized that I'm beautiful inside and out with or without my hair, I was in awe of how strong I am, and I deepened my relationships with everyone. I lost the job I hated. I became an artist. The cancer experience was one of the best things that ever happened to my life."[xxix]

# Day 3:

. . . . . . . . . . . . . . . . . .

## The Sword of Truth

## AFFIRMATION:

*"I am ready to face the Truth about myself and everyone else. And in the hall of mirrors, there is only love."*

Initiation by the sword of truth can be one of the most frightening and enlivening experiences of a lifetime. By Sword of Truth, I mean facing the truth. Sometimes looking in a mirror can be the hardest thing we could ever do.

Finding a person who acts as our mirror—someone who can both see us clearly and tell the truth can be a challenge. Humans have a limited perception mechanism called the body and an ego that protects it, both of which can get in the way of truth. The more someone loves you, really loves you, the more likely they are to be a clear mirror for you. I say "really" loves you because it can take a lot of love, to tell the truth. It also takes courage.

This week, ask five people to answer the following questions about you:

1. What is one thing they admire about you?

2. What do they wish were different about you?

3. What can they count on you for (both good and bad)?

4. What do people say about you when you're not around (both good and bad)?

Feel free to add more questions if you like. Most people will not want to say negative things about you, especially to your face. You will have to make it easier for them by explaining that you are seeking to discover parts of yourself you're not familiar with yet and that whatever they say, you promise not to take it personally. You must stand behind this pledge! You can let them know you value their candor and courage to share freely because it's not easy to see ourselves the way that others see us. Be sure to share your gratitude with them in the end.

After completing this exercise, journal what you learned about yourself. Did you find yourself afraid of hearing what other people thought of you? Did you immediately judge yourself? What were you most afraid they might say? Did you notice any patterns? Did they answer and share from a place of love and concern for you? Did you feel their answers were truthful?

Answer the questions for yourself now, and if you're not sure if your answers are accurate, you can bounce them off friends. You're not limited in time or how many people you ask. This courageous exercise may become something you no longer fear as you choose to care less about what other people think and grow more curious about how you are showing up for others.

We all have our strengths and weaknesses. By identifying both, we have more freedom to choose them consciously instead of unconsciously. It's hard to see how we occur to others unless we ask them. On our journey into self-discovery, we must look in the mirror. Sometimes the best mirror is how others perceive us. The perception of others isn't the "truth" about us, but when it is offered from love, it is a gift of reflection.

# Day 4:

Wielding the Sword of Truth

## AFFIRMATION:

*"The Truth shall set me free. I speak the truth courageously."*

In the previous exercise, you asked others to be a mirror of reflection for you. Now YOU get to be the mirror for others. You have the power to wield the Sword of Truth. First, you must remember how the bear the Sword of Truth by answering 3 questions for yourself:

1. Why wield the Sword of Truth?

2. How do I responsibly wield the Sword of Truth?

3. How do I find the courage to speak my truth?

Why wield the Sword of Truth? Speaking our truth is a large part of why we came here–to this human life on this planet, in this family, at this time. If we fail to speak the truth, we rob the rest of humanity of the opportunity to develop and evolve. Without truth tellers, we cannot trust. Without trust, we have no REAL relationships. Without REAL relationships, our lives are empty and meaningless. Otherwise, we run around pretending that the Emperor is wearing clothes. Truth-telling changes the world and contributes to it.

If I don't tell the truth, I stuff it. If I stuff it, I want to eat emotionally to cover it up, and my thyroid suffers (my truth-telling chakra). If you haven't figured it out yet, truth-telling is foundational to our well-being personally, for the prosperity of our communities and globally as a spiritually evolving species.

How do I responsibly wield the Sword of Truth? Now comes the hardest part. No one has ever given us a class in how to tell the truth responsibly. I do not believe it is responsible to tell the entire truth to everyone ALL the time. There is something to be said for tact, kindness, and timing. Words are powerful and can destroy just like a real sword, depending on the context.

First, we have to determine what IS the Truth that wants to be spoken—to know that, we must first be empty. We must either get our small ego self out of the way or own it. We cannot pretend our personal agenda items are the "Truth" for others. The Truth is not our anger, for example, although our anger may point us in the right direction. Therefore, how I speak the "Truth" should be either that it is only my perception OR that it comes from an inner knowing, from emptiness beyond rational thinking. For the former, I could express myself like, "This is just my personal belief, but it may be helpful, would you like to hear it?" For the latter, I could say something like,

"My inner compass feels uncomfortable with the direction we're going."

If you're not sure where the desire to share your "truth" is coming from, stop. Listen to whether you have emotional charge around it. If so, then it's from your ego. This is an opportunity first to reflect on why your emotional body is so invested in it. Then you might share something like, "I'm feeling angry, and I'm noticing that I want to be right about something, or share something like "By making others wrong, I get to feel better about myself." That's wielding the Sword of Truth on yourself.

Before you wield the Sword of Truth to "cut the crap" away from another human being, I recommend asking permission or waiting for them to ask you for your truth. You might say, "I value our relationship and want to share something with you. I wonder if a good time to talk is now." If they prefer to talk about it later, you might let them know that they're not in trouble, and what you want to share is more about you than them (if that's the case). That is kindness because most people would worry all day as they wait for the "shoe to drop."

I spent most of my life avoiding truth telling for fear of hurting other people's feelings. Now I am learning to be more assertive with my honesty. That is why this step is so important for me, and why I value sharing the truth in a way that it will be heard and will be helpful. I have to remind myself that when I feel that it is time to share the Truth, I must do so regardless of the consequences. It helps tremendously to know my audience before I share so that I can speak their language.

Finally, and most importantly, we must ask ourselves, "Am I sharing this from love? What is my motivating intention here?" The answer is found in our hearts, not in our heads.

My Fairy Godmother once said, "If you're confused, then you're in your head. The heart is never confused." Put your hand on your heart and drop in. This takes a moment of quiet and honest reflection. If I'm sharing something just because I want to look good, then it's not worthy. It usually backfires anyway because other humans can hear the difference between Truth and a show-off. If they think you speak to show-off, they will stop listening. This undermines your power to tell the truth and be heard in the future. I cannot emphasize the value of your word enough.

How do I find the courage to speak the truth? You may fear the consequences of speaking the Truth you know needs telling. Do you remember when Rosa Parks sat at the front of the bus and changed segregation?[xxx] She was speaking her Truth with her actions, and that act must have taken an enormous amount of courage. I aspire to be that courageous.

My homeopathic physician recently gave me a remedy for stage fright. That is one reason I am able to write this book today. I share my truth in hopes that by sharing, I will heal myself and help others to find more freedom. I am hopeful that as more of us share our truths, we will begin to see the bigger perspective from all of our diverse points of view. We must choose courage in the face of fear. Our biology is wired to avoid fearful circumstances or attack them. Courage is a virtue to be summoned, it is like a victory of human spirit. If you want more of it, then you must acknowledge yourself for your courage. Gratitude for anything makes more of it show up. Remember the universe is conspiring to help you. You are never alone. Don't forget to ask for help!

So, where are you still waiting to speak the truth? What stops you? How could you say it diplomatically so that it has the highest chance of being heard?

# Day 5:

. . . . . . . . . . . . . . . . . .

## The Power of Keeping Our Word

## AFFIRMATION:

*"I am powerful. I am my word. You can count on me to keep my word and to immediately restore my integrity when I cannot."*

Nothing is more powerful than our word. Thus far, we have focused on making declarations so that the rest of the universe could conspire with us to create the world we want to live in. Now, it's time to feel our power just by being in alignment with our word.

What if whenever you said something, you could trust that it would actually manifest? What if your life could unfold as you spoke it? This kind of power is available when we become our word. That means we are committed to keeping our word as if it is our most valuable asset. This is called integrity. We can practice this one day at a time until it is our norm. It creates us as trustworthy and reliable.

Let's take being on time for example. Most of us run late quite often. This practice undermines the power of our word. We say that we will get up at 5 am to exercise, but then we change our mind and sleep instead. We don't exercise because we "don't feel like it." This is not a powerful way to live because we will feel like we are always failing.

In my case, I say, "I choose not to eat sugar," and then I break my word, undermining my confidence. If I cannot trust myself to keep my word or my promises, then I cannot trust myself to do anything. If I live from "only if I feel like it," then I am really committed to nothing; I will only accomplish whatever I feel like doing. Feelings change with the wind. I would never have graduated from law school if I let my emotions decide which classes I attended. I had to show up to succeed.

It doesn't matter if the promise is big or small. What is important is that that we do everything in our power to keep our word. This practice also encourages us to be much more careful about to what we give our word. If I say that you can count on me to be somewhere at a specific time, that appointment becomes central to my integrity and the rest of my day revolves around that appointment. If I'm not as committed to that appointment as I am to my ability to help my family if they are ill, then I have to add that possibility to my word. "I'll be there if my father doesn't need me to take him to the doctor."

If something changes on the day of the appointment that gets in the way of my keeping my word, I quickly renegotiate by communicating with all those affected. I might call and let someone know I'm running ten minutes late, for example. If they agree to reset the appointment ten minutes later, then I have restored my integrity as long as this does not become a pattern.

All relationships require integrity to work, especially when it comes to self-confidence. If I could not count on myself to do my homework, I could not have considered going to law school in the first place. If I could not depend on myself to keep my word to pay my mortgage, I could not have considered buying a home. If others cannot rely on me to keep my word, then I'm just a "flake" and not someone with whom they can do business.

Integrity is only available if I consistently keep my word. If I have integrity, then I can be confident in my power to accomplish anything. I want to be able to say, "My life goes a certain way because I say so." How can you be your word today? How can you restore integrity?

# Day 6:

·················

## Discernment

## AFFIRMATION:

*"I am discerning about the character of others and choose to relate to people who are good for me."*

When we feel safe, we don't need to hide. I used to overeat to hide out. Most of us have made the mistake of relating to someone who was not good for us, and we gave our power away. About one in three women and one in four men in this country fall prey to domestic violence, and only 34% of those get the medical care they need to treat the injuries. Many do not survive.[xxxi]

There is great power in discernment. When we embrace this affirmation, it saves us so much unnecessary suffering. Food would not need to be our comforter our sense of control in our lives or our illusion of protection if we embraced this affirmation. Many women would not need to hide behind our baggy clothes.

STEP 9: RECLAIM YOUR POWER

If you are in this boat with so many others, please say today's affirmation over and over. Put it on a post-it on your mirror, frame it on the wall, declare it in your next support meeting, post it on your fridge, and put it everywhere, until you make it wholly and completely a part of your life. Only YOU can take your power back, and the universe is waiting to conspire with you. Please let go of any shame story and ask for help. You are not in this alone! Family, friends, shelters and even strangers would feel privileged to offer you support and freedom if you were willing to transform how you relate to those who are not right for you. Declare that you are done with that old pattern. It does not serve you. You are ready for a life of people who genuinely love you and contribute to you. Yes, that does exist! Your life can be "by invitation only," and you are the one handing out the invitations. Feel free to create physical invitations and hand them out as an exercise of this power.

Your greatest power of discernment is your intuition. Listen to it. Your body will let you know. Your friends and family also have intuition. Listen to them.

Talk to people who have made it through to the other side of this power struggle successfully. Allow them to inspire you—anything is possible.

# Day 7:

........................

## Power Struggles

## AFFIRMATION:

*"I opt out of power struggles."*

Sometimes we don't realize how much energy we waste or how much stress we endure when we are caught up in power struggles. Just thinking about conflict and power struggles makes me want to eat.

Are you a drama queen? Do you allow people to pull you into their dramas? Do you feel exhausted around certain individuals who are always arguing about something or dumping their emotional garbage in your zone? Are you sucked into arguments because they emotionally trigger you and you want to be right? Do you allow others to frame the conversation? Did it occur to you that you may be giving your power away simply by being in the conversation?

A power struggle is often what we call it, when someone creates this kind of dynamic. It's as if there is a game where one person wins, and one loses. A power struggle can only occur if there are at least two people in the conflict. If one person opts out of the struggle, then there isn't one anymore. This is how YOU actually can control your experience if you decide to take your power back—simply remove yourself from the situation.

# HOW DO YOU OPT OUT OF A POWER STRUGGLE?

## First...You must realize that you are in one.

There's an art to identifying a power struggle for what it is while you are in the midst of it. It is often emotionally charged, and it's hard to think when you're upset. So, first, temporarily set aside your emotional reaction and recognize that you are in a power struggle. Here's an example: "Honey, will you turn the TV down, I'm trying to sleep. Some of us have to work for a living!" "Are you saying that you think I should go to work AND raise the children all day as if that's not as difficult a job like yours?" You can hear the unspoken resentments, but instead of sharing them directly, they're creating a power struggle of "I'm right, and you're wrong."

## Second...Make a choice to opt out.

I prefer to opt out almost every time. There are no winners in a power struggle except one person's ego. It's a lot of wasted energy and sometimes destroys the relationship. In this example, one person could literally say, "I hear that you're tired after a long day at work. Would you prefer to sleep now or would you like to share more about your desire that I work outside the home in addition to raising the children." This approach isn't struggling at all. The partner genuinely listened, set aside the initial emotional reaction, and asked more questions to find the underlying cause of it without judgment. It's hard to miscommunicate if you keep asking for clarification.

## Third...Take action to opt out.

Depending on the circumstances, your responses will vary, and I want you to have as much freedom as possible to create something other than a power struggle, especially something unexpected. You might say things like:

♥ *"I'm not interested in having a power struggle with you. Let me know when you are ready to discuss this in a gentle tone."*

♥ *"You are projecting your anger on me, and that doesn't work for me. I'm going to hang up now."*

♥ *Let's set an appointment to discuss this at another time. I need to cool down first."*

♥ *"That's not a conversation I'm willing to have right now. We need to reschedule. Don't call me; I'll call you when I'm ready."*

♥ You can say nothing, just walk away, and not participate.

♥ You can create two bedrooms, one for you and one for your partner. More space can work wonders.

♥  You can let someone know that you need some self-care time and can't be there to support him or her in his or her drama at that moment. Like on an airplane, you may need to put your own oxygen mask on first before assisting others.

♥  You can grab his hand from your buttocks, toss it away from you, and keep talking as if nothing just happened. You can let the other women in the office know to do the same.

♥  You can lie about your name and number and have someone escort you to your car.

♥  You can have a sheriff "standby" while you or your partner could leave the house. Either way, your safety comes first.

♥  You can refuse to vote for any candidate you don't trust, even if it means writing in the name of someone, not on the ballot.

None of these statements has an emotional charge. They are merely stating what you are going to do to meet your needs at that moment. That's why it's not a power struggle. You are not fighting about who is right or wrong anymore. You simply get to say how your life goes. No one else gets to decide for you. You can always walk away. That ability is key to having a healthy relationship. Otherwise, you have no freedom. It's up to you to take your power back.

# STEP 10:

. . . . . . . . . . . . . . . . . .

## *Reconnect*

# WITH YOUR WISDOM

# Day 1:

· · · · · · · · · · · · · · · ·

## Simplicity

## AFFIRMATION:

*"I am wisdom. I simplify."*

Simplicity is a virtue of the archetype of the Wise Woman.[17] Humanity has sought the wisdom of women for thousands of years. In Western Culture, she was known as Athena, the Goddess of Wisdom or the Oracle at Delphi. Even the Kings would consult the wisdom of the Oracle before making important decisions. YOU have that wisdom inside you as well when you stop to listen. Simplicity can help you create the space you need to listen to your own wisdom.

Simplicity even has its own magazine it's so popular.[xxxii] That's because it feels so freeing to have less clutter in our lives, particularly when we're so bombarded by everything else nowadays. One

---

[17] *I'm not saying that men don't also have deep wisdom, but I'm focusing on the Divine Feminine lens that many of us have forgotten how to tap. This inner knowing is intuitive, not rational or logical like the Divine Masculine qualities. See Day 2 of this Step for more.*

way to cope with how fast everything is moving is to have a more peaceful living environment. *If freedom is your goal, having less is having more!* The idea is only to keep that which generates joy for you. When you hold an object or a piece of clothing, ask yourself, "Does it bring me joy?" If not, let it go! Since objects take time to maintain and store, they will deplete our energy unless they also fill us up.

By having a more peaceful living environment, especially a clean one, we feel more peaceful ourselves and less tired, so we reach for food less to cope with our often busy lives. Sometimes I feel so overwhelmed by it all, I want to sit in front of the TV and eat something that comforts me. That just makes things feel worse the next morning! My eyes are puffy, my clothes don't fit, my joints are achy, I'm still tired, and I'm again overwhelmed.

So instead, I could enjoy simplifying one aspect of my life, maybe a closet or a drawer that feels messy, one aspect at a time.

I often feel like "I have nothing to wear" or "nothing fits me." This just makes me feel worse about my body. However, after I clean up my closet and have my clothes mended, I realize I have more than enough to dress beautifully every day, I just forgot what I had in the piles on the floor! I love to hang them up, iron them and sort them by color. An organized, color-coded closet feels like a work of art in itself. The best part is that when I forget how beautiful I am, wearing beautiful clothes lifts my spirits, and everyone around me reminds me.

The hardest thing to simplify for me right now is my finances. I've hired a new bookkeeper to get it all straight in a software program so I can press a button and know precisely where I stand in regards to my budget and my spending. This way, I can limit compulsive buying. It helps that someone else's eyes will see my spending patterns at the end of the month reports. Every receipt adds to my clutter, so I'm looking for ways to simplify, like automatic payments instead of writing checks. I am the possibility of impeccability!

Given my tendency to be a workaholic, the most important question I must answer right now is "How much money do I need each month to feel free?" In other words, how much is enough? Once I answer that question, I must ask, "Who do I need to be or what action am I inspired to take to generate that amount?" Initially, I may need to scrub toilets and make beds. Ultimately, the object of the game is to be paid for things that I REALLY love to do – like creating an online mermaid school.

Make a list of things you would like to simplify and actually calendar one clutter-clearing activity each week so that you have a couple of hours set aside just for that. If it's not on my calendar, it doesn't happen. The faster you organize yourself, the quicker you will feel freer, more joy and more abundance.

# Day 2:

. . . . . . . . . . . . . . . . . .

## Inner Knowingness

## AFFIRMATION:

*"I am deeply connected to my inner knowing. I see clearly and feel the truth."*

Have you ever just known something? Inner knowing is a deep, intuitive knowing. You just **know** it. There is no rationale. There is no logic. There is no left-brain intellectualization. I personally feel this intuition in my belly. It feels like my core knowing. It's a feeling, not a thought. They say that we have brain cells located all over our bodies, not just in the central brain. Perhaps we're tapping into some of those, or maybe we're just listening to the Divine guidance rather than our mental chatter called intelligence.

Most of my life, I've been trained to be intelligent, but seldom in this culture have I been taught to listen to Divine inspiration. That would be valuable because Divine Will does not always comply with the ideas of the rational, logical, analytical brain. I value the logical part of my brain for survival and strategy, but not as a compass for my life's purpose.

The truth is, we ALL have a pineal gland in the center of our brain (also called the third eye), and it works like antennae to tap into knowledge beyond our limited thinking. So why haven't we all learned to use this gland on a daily basis?

If we connect to our inner knowing, then others cannot control us with untruths or propaganda. It is in the interest of some to keep most of us from connecting to our truth. Those who want to control others (such as big tobacco or the sugar association) do not want us to connect to our inner knowing, and they have mastered the art of marketing to us. Our consumer-driven culture sells us depleted processed food, beauty products we don't need and prescription drugs to cover up symptoms. They bombard us with a message that we need to consume more and more of everything.

So, how do you drown out all the marketing and tap into your inner knowing? Start by turning off the commercials. Do you hear your knowing auditorily? Do you see it (visual learner)? Do you feel it in your body? Do you remember a time when you listened to your intuition? Do you remember how doing so saved you from making a poor decision? How can you learn to trust this gift and develop it more?

Try applying your inner knowing to your food choices—"will this food nourish me?" Try applying it to the rest of your choices:

- ❤ **REST**—"Should I get up early to exercise or do I need more rest?"

- ❤ **EXERCISE**— "Is this the kind of exercise that works for my body today or shall I take a different approach?"

- ❤ **WORK**—"Does this work bring me joy or am I just here to pay the rent?"

- ❤ **ROMANTIC RELATIONSHIP**—"Does this person inspire me or does he/she deplete me?"

Why not apply this approach to everything. We often seek the answers outside of ourselves by asking friends, family or experts. Honestly, I think we do this, even though we already know the answer, but we don't want to hear it! Who wants to hear that traditional ice cream isn't the best approach to a healthy dinner? Even experts aren't always right. What if YOU are the expert in knowing when you can listen deeply?

It's critical for each of us to know the difference between inner knowing and our mental conversations because one aspect of addiction is mental. We have to be able to observe our mental process and say, "Oh, that's just my brain telling me that. That's not the truth, it's an old tape playing that likes to beat me up." Now, when I hear my brain say, "That's bad for you! You're a bad person for eating that," I can reply, "Thank you for sharing, and now I choose to eat this glorious food as it nourishes me and I am grateful for my beautiful body and how wonderful I am!"[18] Write down some of your affirmations on a card and try saying one that you like next time you hear the mental abuse begin.

---

[18] *Emotional Freedom Technique (EFT) works great here too!*

# Day 3:

......................

## Just ACT Like You're Sober!

## AFFIRMATION:

*"My life flows from inspired action. Everything is available to me when I choose to experience it NOW. I can BE anything I desire at any time."*

Yesterday, after two cookies, two bags of chips and a marshmallow treat, I spoke with my wise support coach, Randy Mitchell.[19] He said, "Just act like you're sober." The wisdom of this mindset got me out of my slump and back on track immediately. The best part is that it applies to everything in my life!

It's the idea that if I **BE** the person that I desire first, the rest follows. If you want to be a millionaire, you just act like one, and the money must follow. If you desire to be a mermaid, you just act like one, and the magic must follow. If you want to be a person of impeccable integrity, you just act like one. In this case, I want to be healthy and vital and someone who cares about her beautiful body.

---

[19] *I recommend Weight Management University with Randy at http://avarlifestyle-wmu.com.*

So I am, NOW, at this moment! From this new mindset, I make my food choices, and I guarantee you that junk food is not invited to the party.

That means I don't have to wait for the stars to align to have what I want. It works the other way around. I visualize my art room painted the color that I desire, with the supplies that I need and creative projects happening, and allow myself to see it, as already done feeling the joy that comes with that. When I experience aspects of my life this way the universe steps in. My visualization happens by the universe inspiring others and myself to take action.

Inspired action, according to my coach, is the inspiration for action that bubbles up from the spirit, and you should not be confused with the analytical mind. My mind wanted to insert itself when he asked me, *"How would your life look if you had no doubt about anything?"* He reminded me to get my mind out of the way (that's a good rule of thumb for soul questions).

I found myself dreaming up a desire for more abundance of time, money, beauty, art, music, joy and laughter, mindfulness, rest, spiritual reflection, stopping to smell the roses, and magic. I couldn't help smiling the whole time.

My vision got more specific. I imagined my mermaid school as a magical oasis where people from all over the world playfully discover their gifts and reconnect with who they really are. Mermaids are limitless and abundant, and so are humans when they allow themselves to think outside the box. I remember feeling stuck at my desk job and wondering how I would ever find time or energy to play again in the sun, in the ocean or hula-hoop in the rain. I used to work all year (sixty hours a week) to earn one-week vacation in Hawaii. Now I am paid to be a mermaid, to play with people in the sun and the ocean every day. You know you've arrived when you don't think about vacations anymore because there is no place you'd rather be.

The most important thing I remembered today was to *experience* the wisdom that I seek to embody, not just intellectualize it. You could read this book repeatedly as an intellectual exercise, and it may not change your life. In contrast, you could *experience* even one sentence of this book, and that experience could transform your life forever.

Once I experience wisdom in my body, it feels real! Then, if I encounter it repeatedly, I know it's real, and it becomes a habit. That new habit replaces old ones that no longer serve me. Now, I base my life on these new beliefs instead of the ones I made up in childhood.

Everyone should have a wisdom coach, not because we don't have the wisdom inside of us, but because we often can't find the keys. How often do you lose your car keys and ask for help? That's what a wisdom coach does. If you don't hire help, find a buddy that can help you remember your wisdom by asking the right questions when you've "lost your keys."

# Day 4:

. . . . . . . . . . . . . . . . . .

## The Value of Humor

## AFFIRMATION:

*"Stop being your own worst enema!"*

Want to lose weight? Yes, you CAN laugh your ass off!

Laughter is one of our most excellent medicines. In fact, we can make fun of this entire addictive lesson! Why wallow in the mud when we can sling it and make a game of the messiness of life. Let's stop taking the whole thing so seriously and start to joke about it. Since it doesn't mean anything about us anymore, we're free to make fun of ourselves.

This Step finds wisdom in humor. In some indigenous cultures, it's called coyote-wisdom and is brought to you by the "wise woman." She's a crone of a different color who smacks you on the head with her staff and speaks in "crazy" wisdom when she wants you to wake up! If that happens, be sure to listen.

I'm not suggesting making fun of our obesity – fat jokes are painful for most humans. There's plenty to laugh about without needing to offend anyone. I'm recommending that we make fun of our own behaviors as much as possible. The more we can release our ego and the disempowering meanings we assign to our stories, the freer we become! Aside from the side effect of belly laughs, connection, intimacy, and joy, it's just plain fun! Additionally, humor can crack our stories open when we least expect it. It's like therapy through ecstasy rather than making it "hard."

Make a list of some of your "crazy" behaviors around food and body image. Speak of them as if they're in the past and make fun of them as if they're old friends. Here are a few of mine:

- ♥ I used to plan dinner before I was done with breakfast.

- ♥ I was so afraid there wasn't going to be enough food that if someone reached toward my plate, I would hug it closer and eat faster. You knew I loved you if I offered you a bite of anything.

- ♥ I used to hide a box of candy under my bed and sneak it whenever I could. My life was about buying secret candy.

- ♥ I even tried bulimia once or twice, but couldn't make it work. I was too afraid people would find out.

- ♥ I used to eat a whole bag of chips while grocery shopping before I even made it to the checkout.

It's fun to distinguish the old behaviors that still show up from time to time—so I can laugh at them and create new habits in their place.

When I feel resigned, humor helps break up how serious I'm being. It's insane to think that candy bars are in control of my life! Imagine me have an arm wrestling match with a candy bar—literally. If I continue to eat mac and cheese every night for dinner, I'll soon replace the couch instead of the person sitting on it. If I keep sitting on the couch, I might forget how to get up, and if I can't get up, I won't be able to reach the chocolate. Now, that's a problem!

Try to find humor in everything to take your power back from the negative self-talk. Find cartoons, collect jokes, watch funny movies, and hang with funny people, all to break the old patterns. Start sharing them on our Facebook page.

# Day 5:

. . . . . . . . . . . . . . . .

## Dualistic Reality–What's Real?

### AFFIRMATION:

*"I am bigger than right or wrong, good or bad. I am whole, perfect and complete, just like everyone else."*

I was on a boat today to help snorkelers in the ocean. I was dressed as a mermaid and telling stories about how many fish in the sea are hermaphrodites, changing sex when needed. I said the ocean was the largest transgender bathroom in the world.[xxxiii] Given today's politics, some people laughed and appreciated the humor, others pretended it was comfortable, and others put their hands over their children's ears.

When you listen to the opinion of others, do you ask in your mind, "Do I agree or disagree" to decide whether to listen anymore?

In the past, everything was either good or bad, black and white, right or wrong. This especially applied to food for me. I felt resentful and limited that I was only allowed to eat "good for me food." That felt like a diet against which I wanted only to rebel. However, I felt guilty and ashamed when I ate "bad for me" food. Either way, I always lost the battle I had started with good food versus bad food.

Why would I make up such a no-win story? I did so because I organized my entire life as good and bad. I applied the same story to everything and everyone. I had to be a "good girl" and avoid "bad" things growing up. This story had me feeling suicidal at age eight for experimenting with sexuality. Some of us make up that we're "bad" deep down, usually because we're told that at an early age. Our entire life then responds to us as if we're unworthy.

What dualistic stories do you tell yourself about food, about you and about life in general? Are you stuck in the story of "right" and "wrong?" This assumes there's only one-way to do something and is especially popular for those who want to know how to get to heaven. In the midst of addiction, we create living hell here and now. In freedom, like a seed, we grow.

Dualistic thinking is one of the most limiting belief systems we could ever choose to play out in our lives. So, why would we choose it? The benefit is the comfort that we gain from believing that we are on the right path. When we are the "chosen ones" and feel special, life seems a little less scary and uncertain. Black and white thinking makes the world feel safer. Of course, this is just an illusion since this kind of thinking is what makes it easy to go to war. It's easier to war against others if they're "evil" and we're "good." In fact, it's impossible to kill others if we fail to villainize them first. Do not judge yourself or others for dualistic thinking. It is a crutch in a fearful world. If we address the underlying fear, the limited thinking will begin to soften and disappear itself.

Identify where this kind of thinking limits your experience of life, of food, of passion, of joy, of friendship. How would a conversation go if you weren't filtering out the "bad" stuff? How would a relationship go with food if you weren't judging everything on your plate? How would your relationships with others go if you weren't judging everyone all the time? Try it out. Expand. Risk a little. The world may feel safer when we have more room for each other. Living in the gray areas instead of only the black or white areas may feel a little uncomfortable at first. Everyone around you will relax more if you do.

# Day 6:

. . . . . . . . . . . . . . . . . .

## The Refrigerator Problem

## AFFIRMATION:

*"I am noble. I am a Queen. To be of service to others, I must regularly refill my own gas tanks."*

I can't tell you how many times I have felt unworthy to have my own needs met and then resentful when others want something from me.

Maiden, Mother, Crone: These are the three phases of a woman's life. The world responds to women differently depending on in which phase we are. The problem with being in the "Mother" phase is that much of our family has become **accustomed to treating us like a refrigerator.** They assume that whenever they are hungry for food, attention, clean laundry, or a ride somewhere, they can just metaphorically open the door to the refrigerator and take whatever they want from the mother. The children and spouse often learn to feel entitled to this and take it for granted. The problem with this approach is that it can quickly leave anyone playing this role exhausted.

You don't have to be a crone to have wisdom and boundaries. There are other possibilities available. By embodying the archetype of the queen, for example, you may find that motherhood is more sustainable. Queens are like mothers in that they serve their people, providing much wisdom, prosperity, guidance, and protection. However, a queen also allows herself to be treated royally, never to be taken for granted or treated like a refrigerator.

A queen carves out time for fulfilling her own dreams, her spa day, her personal health and wellness. She knows that her service is only possible if she is not depleted. She often has "knights" who serve HER. She may have a partner or a whole village that supports her. Embodying the queen is an attitude that values who you are in essence and how much you contribute to others. She commands respect because she respects herself.

What's great about this possibility is that it is entirely within your control. You get to make up the rules about how others will approach you. Embodying the queen is something YOU decide to be, and to which others respond. This may be a new experience for those around you so it may take some time to retrain your family members to treat you differently than before. They may be accustomed to your making their lunches every day, for example. Now, it may be time for THEM to learn to make their own sandwiches or to do the laundry. Give yourself permission to be treated royally as you continue to love your family. You can treat them royally too, but not in a sacrificial way. If you have to get up every two hours to breast-feed, then you're going to need a lot of support! Ask for help and let yourself have it!

You deserve it when you're Queen. Being queen is merely a reflection of your Divine nobility. Being a queen doesn't mean you're better than others in a hierarchy are. We are all noble creations. Wise royalty knows their lives are of service to their people, but they also know to treat themselves well so they can continue to play that role.

Fake it 'till you make it. Just BE the Queen today and see how it goes. ***You may be surprised to find that you enchant others.*** This archetype also works well for the maiden years. When dating, sometimes the masculine relates to the maiden as fun to date, but not necessarily marriage material. If you want someone to relate to you as more than just a good time, you will have to step into your Queen-energy and command respect.[xxxiv]

# Day 7:

· · · · · · · · · · · · · · · ·

## Embrace the Paradox

## AFFIRMATION:

*"I am a victory of the human spirit, free to choose my reality even when it feels like a paradox."*

To embrace paradox is to hold two seemingly opposing concepts at the same time. Paradox is often confusing to our logical brains. The willingness to stay in paradox takes courage. For example, most of Europe uses homeopathy as energy medicine. The concept is that our bodies get used to chronic symptoms and our immune system may forget that they are even foreign anymore. By giving our body a dose of something that would typically cause all those same symptoms, it reminds the body that it should heal itself. It's a paradox that we make the symptoms worse temporarily to trigger the body to respond with its immune system. Homeopathy has not caught on as well in America because we want a pill that will take away all the symptoms immediately, even if only temporarily.

The result is that we never actually heal the underlying problem. Instead, we just cover it up.

The most recent election of Donald Trump is also a paradox. From the conservative perspective, he is able to speak to the fears of many Americans, particularly to the religious right and promote corporate prosperity. Since we live in a culture where prejudice is still very much alive, many Americans feel they must hide their prejudice to be politically correct. From that perspective, it is refreshing that Trump speaks his mind rather than pretending not to be racist, sexist, anti-Muslim, or "fatist." Unlike many of us, he is at least honest when he speaks unscripted.

From a more liberal perspective, Trump's behavior has been a homeopathic remedy making these symptoms worse at first, so that America can become inspired to heal its divides of race, gender, and unregulated corporate greed.

From my inner three-year-old's perspective, Trump can appear as a father figure promising security and money—a father that most Americans have never had given our country's 50% divorce rate. Marketing principal #1 assumes our emotions drive most human decisions, and from that perspective, the election results should not surprise us.

What is most interesting about the Trump paradox is how we have refused to embrace it, creating division and violence. We can hardly even speak of it to each other if we come from differing perspectives. Embracing paradox is not easy. It takes courage and maturity. It takes a willingness to sit uncomfortably within our own rigid ideas. It requires a softening, a humility and a willingness not to have to be right always. Are you willing to give up being right to have peaceful relationships with others?

The great Sufi poet, Rumi[xxxii], said,

*"Out beyond ideas of wrong-doing and right-doing, there is a field. I'll meet you there. When the soul lies down in that grass, the world is too full to talk about. Ideas, language, even the phrase, each other doesn't make any sense."[xxxv]*

So, how does paradox relate to food addiction? I find it paradoxical to believe that there is nothing wrong and nothing to fix in the face of a sugar hangover. It seems illogical to believe that if I focus on creating what I DO want in my life, the things I DON'T want will naturally fall away without effort. I find it a challenge to trust that the healing process itself may require me to reopen a wound and feel the pain first so my physical cells can feel safe to release all the protection I currently carry. I find it paradoxical that I may need to soften and become more vulnerable to feel safer, or that safety and survival aren't why we're here at all.

My biology is wired one way—and my spirit seems to be wired another. The ability to choose a victory of human spirit over my mechanical reactions is the name of the game. It is where real freedom lies. It is where heaven on earth becomes possible. Given that our biological minds are limited, embracing paradox is the only way through the eye of the needle.

Life isn't black and white, right or wrong, good or bad. Dualistic thinking is a stage of our early development, one we must grow out of when we enter our wisdom years. We teach small children dualistic concepts because it helps keep them safe, but we must not become stuck there. We didn't come here to play safe. Have courage and give yourself this gift. Where do you still struggle with paradox? Stop struggling. Both may be true.

# STEP 11:

. . . . . . . . . . . . . . . . . .

# Connection

# Day 1:

· · · · · · · · · · · · · · · ·

## I Am Already Connected

## AFFIRMATION:

*"I am loved and supported by thousands of years of wisdom woven into a net created by my ancestors. It is in my blood, in my DNA."*

By acknowledging your lineage, you will feel more connected to your ancestors. Lift your left arm up and say, "I love my mother. I love my mother's mother. I love my mother's, mother's, mother and all the way back to the beginning of time." Now, lift your right arm straight up and say, "I love my father. I love my father's father. I love my father's father's father and all the way back to the beginning of time."[xxxvi]

Just as you love them, they love you. Let that in for a moment. Feel it. Your ancestors have been weaving a web of support under you your entire life to catch you when you fall, to provide what you need, to protect you. Feeling that web of support can make a huge difference in our well-being.

There are three steps to connect more with our ancestors:

1. **ACKNOWLEDGE THAT THEY STILL EXIST,** although not in physical form. Some traditions, like in Japan, create a sacred space for a family photo, light a candle and display favorite objects, flowers, etc., to honor the ancestors. It is similar to how we place flowers and headstones on graves.

2. **ASK FOR THEIR HELP.** Our ancestors are waiting behind the veil to help, but the laws of the universe do not allow them to "meddle" in our lives unless we ask. Practice saying, "Help," more often. You might ask them to sit on your life's "wisdom counsel" so you can consult with them from time to time. Imagine if you passed over, wouldn't you still want to be involved in the lives of those you loved. In the unseen world, there is no limitation of time, space or money.

3. **THANK THEM.** Gratitude is the key to maintaining all relationships and to offering reciprocity.

Why limit yourself to your direct lineage? Open up the request for help to all beings who are in your favor. Sometimes it's hard to remember that we are all cousins. Even if only by the fiftieth degree, all the human family is related. Therefore, if we go back far enough, my ancestors are also your ancestors. That means all of your heroes are also related to you. That's right; both Eleanor Roosevelt AND Gene Wilder are related to you. Of course, our Higher Power is always here for us too, not to mention our guardian angels and spirit guides.

Since I've moved to Hawai'i, I've come to appreciate having a guide more than ever before. It's an entirely different experience to go into the ocean with no guidance than to have someone show me. I would see about 90% less without a guide. I wouldn't know where the rip currents are when the jellies bloom, or where to enter safely. I wouldn't know where the sharks sleep, what a fish cleaning station is or where the most beautiful "swim-throughs" are. Life works the same way. Why go it alone, when all of this guidance is available to us if we ask for it.

The experience of having a well-woven web of love under me is like no other. Having grown up without financial security, it means everything for me to feel that I have something to fall back on. I know my ancestors have been weaving their support under me forever, as I have done for others. It feels like a trampoline on which I can jump and play, and even if I fall through the cracks, they will catch me. This sense of security creates a very different experience of life for me—one that is not motivated primarily by survival mode. Ironically, sometimes I think my Norwegian ancestors want me to eat more potatoes and put a little weight on because that is what worked for them in the cold northern winters. When this craving comes, I thank them and make my own choices in spite of their good intentions.

By feeling this connectedness, I am less likely to reach for food to fulfill me or to comfort me when I feel afraid. There is total support for fulfilling my dreams.

# Day 2:

. . . . . . . . . . . . . . . . . .

## Choosing Your Community

## AFFIRMATION:

*"I am not alone. I am an important part of a loving community—a tribe of my own choosing."*

Whether you already have a family or need to create your own, surrender to the idea that you are part of a community. Connecting to others intimately is your choice. That may require you to give up some old fears of abandonment or commitment. Journal about what still keeps you feeling separate from others.

We live in the cult of individualism in America—where everyone is expected to leave their communities at age eighteen and act like our ancestors who came to this country with very little support. This is not who we really are. Humans are social beings and live in groups. We usually live cooperatively because it works. If you could easily release your addictive patterns all by yourself, you wouldn't be reading this book right now—and it makes it one million times harder to do this alone. You didn't get these addictive patterns all by yourself—our media, our culture, and our families gave these habits to us. Therefore, it will be easier to release them with a team approach.

For some of us (myself included) this is scary—to think that we may need other people, or that asking for support may feel like a burden to others and they will pull away. The opposite is true. Vulnerability brings others closer, more intimate, and you can receive assistance lavished upon you. That's why prayer is so powerful—the universe loves it when we ask for help—it's been waiting to lavish us with support—but we have to open to it first.

# AN EXERCISE

Draw who your community is now using three circles—your family and closest friends that you could call upon for support at any time. Draw a circle for each of your circles of influence, such as a church or fellow employees/colleagues. Draw a circle for those you may not have even considered yet such as angelic support, a 13 Step support circle, a book club, photography or poetry meet up, etc.

This is a 13 Step Program and must include your full participation in a community of 13 Steppers to carry you through when you need support as an individual. Being part of a broader community also allows you to support others and to get out of yourself. Consider that you are not the center of the universe—a key to healing addictive patterns. The relationship of support is symbiotic—it goes both ways. If you are an over-giver, then your job is to learn to receive more and actively ask for support. If you tend to receive more than you give, it's time to practice generosity and read my favorite children's book "The Quilt Maker."[xxxvii]

Did you know that "who you know?" determines how 75% of jobs are obtained? Since I never felt I had any connections, I always thought I had to get a job on the merits. I thought it took "hard work." Later I learned that I could continue to work hard and be poor or I could hardly work and be rich. It's all just a story we make up about how the universe works!

After having been an employer for almost twenty years, I realized that I hired first for attitude, not for skill (since the latter can be taught). I hired because someone's heart was in it—because working with me fulfilled his or her dream. I wanted to be around people who cared for and contributed to others. My law clients hired me because I genuinely cared for them, not because of what school I attended, my awards or what fees I charged. The reason it's important to realize this is that, when we do, our dream job becomes available. Why spend a lifetime performing tasks that do not light you up? Yes, only limited thinking stands in the way. When was the last time you felt lit-up? How could you be compensated for doing whatever lights you up?

Now, say the affirmation again,

*"I am an important part of a loving community—a tribe of my own choosing."*

Journal how you will consciously choose the community you desire. Whom will you choose to be your family, friends, work colleagues, playmates, team, or conspirators?

# Day 3:

Creating Your Support Team

## AFFIRMATION:

*"I surround myself with a powerful support team that uplifts and inspires me."*

This practical step is not based on the past. You must choose your support team from the future. First, imagine where you are going. Whom you will need to get there will be informed. Do not base your team on past experience. Who will you need to support you in obtaining your visioned future?

For myself, I choose the following team players:

- ♥ A romantic partner who provides daily affection

- ♥ A business partner and employees who contribute to my financial well-being

- ♥ A 13 Step support group

- ♥ A good doctor and homeopath

- ♥ A massage therapist

- ♥ A buddy who keeps me accountable for my food journal

- ♥ A naturopath who provides supplement and nutrition advice

- ♥ A life coach to keep me on track toward fulfilling my dreams

- ♥ A gentle dentist

- ♥ An exercise buddy, team or coach of some kind

- ♥ A Faerie Godmother

- ♥ A small group of personal friends with whom I can share

- ♥ A group of wonderful guests at my bed & breakfast

I made a list of my team members and set appointments with each of them. Consider making your appointments. What are you waiting for? I recommend that you do not leave an appointment without setting your next appointment, so the support keeps coming. If you are having a limiting conversation about whether you can afford your team players, please repeat the abundance exercises on Day 6 of Step 4 and Day 5 of Step 5 (extra abundance) or at least fake it for now. I believe in your ability to manifest whatever you desire. You are a powerful creator whether you know it yet or not.

# Day 4:

## Self-Care Plan

### AFFIRMATION:

*"I do a great job of taking care of my body. I appreciate how strong, flexible and vibrant my body is!"*

Learning new habits about how to provide support to my physical body requires me to come up with a Self-care Plan. This beautiful body is on loan to me, and its maintenance is 100% my responsibility. We have a three-thousand-mile plan for my car lube and oil, why not calendar my own body tune-ups. What healthy habits do you need in place for optimum performance? Here's what I want in my daily routine:

♥ **I DRINK EIGHT TO TEN GLASSES OF PURE WATER DAILY**— distilled and filtered—drinking them slowly throughout the day. I often add some lemon or apple cider vinegar.

- ♥ **I EAT FIVE SMALL MEALS**, one every three hours starting upon waking. If I'm losing weight, then I only eat enough to last me about two hours, so the last hour I feel slightly hungry, not famished. This allows me to gently burn fat throughout the day without going into starvation mode. If my body thinks I'm dieting, then it feels stressed and burns muscle instead of fat.

- ♥ **I TRY TO STABILIZE MY CORTISOL LEVELS.**[xxxviii] I eat more protein (fewer carbs) in my early meals and my evening meal has more carbs (fewer proteins.)

- ♥ **I EAT WHOLE, ORGANIC FOODS** (not processed).

- ♥ **I BALANCE MY FOOD PH.** I eat 80% alkaline foods and 20% acidic foods. That means mostly veggies. I don't eat completely raw foods because my spleen isn't ready for that. I often blanch my vegetables before I blend them into soup in the Vitamix, so my body doesn't have to work as hard to break them down.

- ♥ **I COMBINE MY FOODS CAREFULLY** by type, so I don't eat fruit with meat for example. I don't mix carbs and proteins. I eat melon alone.[20]

- ♥ **I EXERCISE THIRTY TO SIXTY MINUTES A DAY.**

- ♥ **I SLEEP AS MUCH AS I NEED.** That means going to bed around 9 p.m., not setting the alarm clock and naturally waking up rested at about 5 a.m. I take a nap when I need it.

---

[20] I learned this from the Optimum Health Institute, San Diego, California.

♥ **I CREATE SPIRITUAL TIME** from 5 a.m. to 6 a.m. to center my soul and feel inspired to step fully into my mythic life. Without this, my spiritual amnesia sets in, and I forget who I am and why I'm here.

♥ **I GET IN THE WATER AT LEAST ONCE A DAY.** I try to get in the ocean daily, or at least take a shower, if not a bath. I am like a fountain and water is my refill station.

♥ **I HAVE COME TO AVOID ANIMAL PROTEIN** during the writing of this book, and in the end, dropped twenty-five pounds and four dress sizes. I now prefer not to eat meat unless it is treated kindly and grown sustainably. Sustainable also means that they do not seriouly harm the land. Cattle in the rainforest does not work if we want to breathe oxygen in the future. I do not eat tuna, marlin, swordfish, shark or any other large fish because we have already killed 90% of them—not to mention their mercury content. I grew up fishing with my father and loved it. However, I believe the large fishing industry continues to devastate our oceans and its creatures. I support the small fishing traditions as long as they act responsibly toward other creatures by not harming dolphins, whales, seals, and turtles. I will boycott any fisherman who operates otherwise, such as those in Taiji, Japan that slaughter over 1000 dolphins every year.[xxxix]

♥ **I PLAY.** I avoid stress by replacing it with play. Even being a lawyer can be treated like a game. Whenever I feel stress, my body switches to the sympathetic nervous system and begins to burn muscle instead of fat. That means I listen to beautiful music or meditate to bring me back to the para-sympathetic nervous system.

- ♥ **I AVOID CHEMICALS** and pollutants including sugar and alcohol. That includes not using chemicals in my beauty supplies, home or on my clothes. I avoid prescription drugs unless absolutely necessary.

- ♥ **I TAKE SUPPLEMENTS** to assist with high-quality nutrition.

- ♥ **I FREQUENTLY CLEANSE** inside too. That includes gentle food cleanses and regular colon hydrotherapy or enemas until I'm "regular" again.

Now, I have to schedule whatever activities are necessary to support this plan. I calendar time to go grocery shopping each week as well as food preparation. I calendar exercise and spiritual time. I make sure I go to bed on time, so I can stay on track. I can move the schedule around anytime, so it remains flexible.

So what are the pillars of your self-care plan? Write them down. Share them with your support team and ask for help with implementation. My spouse, for example, does the grocery shopping, so I don't have to look at 90% of the food in the store that I choose not to eat. We take turns cooking and communicate about what works and doesn't work for our health and wellbeing. Stay on track each week using a Vitality Chart similar to mine (See Exhibit G).

# Day 5:

· · · · · · · · · · · · · · · · ·

## Exercise

## AFFIRMATION:

*"I LOVE to exercise my strong and flexible body, and it loves me!"*

Daily exercise is critical for everyone. Our ancestors were nomadic initially, only settling down for agriculture a couple thousand years ago. The point is that our bodies are made to move! I use low impact exercises like restorative yoga, swimming, walking, or gentle circuit training. If I exercise strenuously for more than eight seconds, activity in my parasympathetic nervous system decreases and increases in my sympathetic nervous system, which in turn burns muscle instead of fat. Hence, short sprints are better than endurance runs for what I want to accomplish. I believe in moderation, not extreme sports like marathons.

Moderation isn't an adrenaline rush, and that's why it works for me. Have you ever met an overweight yogini? "Overweight" isn't real, it's just a story. I could also say "under-tall," "Rubenesque," "voluptuous," "weight challenged," or "extra fluffy." I'm a mermaid from the northern tribes where having some extra padding helps keep us warm, especially in water. One of my friends claims to be from the whale family. If we assume the body knows exactly what it needs at all times, then we fall off the judgment wagon! You wouldn't let anyone else call you fat, yet what do you say to yourself when you look in the mirror?

Sitting for more than 45 minutes is toxic. Get up and move around. Stretch, sing, laugh or connect with others. Get a desk that converts to standing. We were not meant to sit all day. I elevate my legs at night to bring the blood back more easily. I sleep on an amethyst biomat to support my thyroid. I love jumping on my tiny trampoline to get my lymph moving a couple times a day. I love brushing my skin for the same reason. I love turning on happy music and dancing around with my hula-hoop! When it's hot outside, I turn on the sprinkler and exercise in the faux rain—I call it "sprinklercises."

You can sign up for horseback riding, team sports, classes at the gym, walk the beach every day, find a meetup group for bird watching and walking or go dancing one night a week. Ideally, you wouldn't even know you were exercising because you would be having so much fun!

Make a list of your favorite action activities and calendar them. Need help to get motivated? Create an event in the future that you want to be ready for—like fitting in a bikini for a trip to Hawaii. If you always have something to shoot for, it will make it easier to get off the couch. If the sofa keeps calling you, lose it! That goes for the TV too. I cover mine with a pretty scarf and put flowers in front of it. If something newsworthy occurs, I'm sure I'll see it online.

Explore things you've never done before. You don't have to like them, just try them. You might like archery or scuba diving or hang gliding. Pull out the old canoe and get on the water this weekend! If you don't enjoy yourself, sell the canoe. Buy some roller blades and go to the park. Go bowling or find a meetup group that wants to take photos of the flowers in your neighborhood. Just find active ways to have a good time. You're more likely to exercise if you actually enjoy it.

# Day 6:

. . . . . . . . . . . . . . . . . . . .

## Your Favorite Foods

## AFFIRMATION:

*"By planning ahead, I have even more freedom—freedom to choose from all the healthy delicious meals I recently prepared."*

Let's move to the nitty-gritty details now. This is the part I resist the most—creating a food plan. I fear that once I create a plan, I will feel trapped by it. I want to feel free to eat whatever I want whenever I want.

For a food plan to work for me, it must have three critical ingredients:

1. Taste good
2. Be nutritious
3. Be flexible

Make a list of things you like to eat that are also nutritious and fit the values of your Self-Care Plan. Ideally, create a recipe book or binder that has photos of these foods. This will be your at-home-menu—the greater the variety, the better.[21] There are excellent meal planning applications now available free on the internet, for example, I recommend "Forks Over Knives."[xl]

Set aside time once a week to choose a few dishes from your menu and pick up enough groceries to cook for the entire week. Only prepare enough food to cover the meals you'll need for the next 3 days. When that food is gone, cook enough meals for the next three days, and so on. Some people love to freeze meals for later.

When I first started this practice, I hired a personal chef to help me come up with meals that actually tasted good.[xli] Alternatively, you could ask your friends to come over and bring their favorite recipes once a month. I had never learned to cook before. Making friends with food is the goal here.

To know what I needed at the grocery store, I had to write up a meal plan for the week. I would feel resentful when I wanted to go out to eat, and my husband would say, "Honey, we need to eat the food in the fridge, or it will go bad." This triggered my emotional body to want to rebel and never cook anything again! Therefore, I shared my dilemma with him, and he said that I was entirely free to eat what and when I chose, and even to waste food. That last bit was hard for him because he was raised never to waste food. He eats everything on his plate. It's funny how our childhood food trauma plays out 44 years later.

---

[21] You can also get to go menus from your favorite restaurants and highlight the items that fit your Self-Care Plan. That way you'll know where you can find nutritious food that tastes good.

The most important part for me in food preparation is the beautification! The plate must be beautiful! I can't tell you how many sets of dishes I own. I always use a linen napkin because it reminds me "I'm worth it." I even bring a tablecloth, pretty napkin, real silverware and a flower in my car for fast food emergencies. It changes the entire experience when I eat at a not-so-lovely restaurant with such lovely amenities! If you pack your lunch, you can do the same. In most of Europe, they don't need permission to enjoy the beauty of their food. They simply expect high quality. Americans have much to learn in that department. Do not skimp on the quality of your food.

# Day 7:

## Physical Touch

## AFFIRMATION:

*"Touch is a beautiful thing. I powerfully stand for everyone's boundaries, so touching is safe."*

We are all here to feel connected, so everyone should know their primary love language.[xli] There are five to choose from:

1. Touch

2. Acts of Service

3. Gifts

4. Words of Affirmation

5. Quality Time

Of these, my primary love language is "touch." That means it doesn't matter how often you tell me you love me or how many gifts you bring me or how much time we spend together, I won't know that you love me if you don't touch me. Without touch, babies die. We all need it, even when we get older. We cannot be healthy without affectionate touch. It is like drinking water, we must have touch.

We can get a massage, ask for hugs, or request affection from others. In college, I used to believe that I couldn't ask for affection without "going all the way" because someone once told me that would make me "a tease." That's a very limiting belief and a disempowering story. We can all have exactly what we want within the boundaries that we specify. Boundaries are an excellent tool for safety. Safety makes intimacy possible.

Most cultures are not afraid of non-sexual touch as we are here in America. It is often customary for people in other cultures to hold hands, lock arms and hug each other all the time, especially in the Mediterranean. Having lived in Istanbul for a year, I really enjoyed this kind of regular touch among my host family and friends.

We can share touch with our pets, with the ground by taking our shoes off on the earth, or by getting in the water and allowing it to caress our skin. However, you like to be touched, make it happen! It's not just good for you, it's necessary for our well-being. If we don't get touch, we may reach for food or other addictions to fill this need instead. Many of us often mistake food for love.

Make a list of the kind of touch you enjoy and who you can ask to provide it. If you are not getting enough touch, then practice asking for more. Others are probably wanting more too and would be thrilled to provide it. Touch is fulfilling.

# STEP 12:
............

## *Release*

# Day 1:

. . . . . . . . . . . . . . . .

## Letting Go

AFFIRMATION:

*"I release anything that no longer serves me. It is done! Thank you."*

It is time to **let go of that, which no longer serves you**. On a fresh piece of paper, make a list of what no longer serves you. Here are some places to look: addictive behaviors; extra weight; self-destructive behaviors; old relationships (old lovers/marriages); sadness; anger and resentment; self-sabotage; depression[22]; fear (be specific); or disempowering stories of betrayal. More places to look are hopelessness; resignation; negative thinking; lack of trust; disease; pain; discomfort; old clothes or furnishings; negative emotions or the desire to control others.

One of the most life-changing questions someone ever asked me was, "Why are you married?" The fact that I could not answer the question several years ago was telling. I had either to recreate

---

[22] *I've attached my journal entry of my journey into depression as Exhibit H if it helps.*

my first marriage or let it go. The dynamics of my first marriage were depleting me, so after fifteen years of struggling with exhaustion and limiting beliefs about marriage, I gave myself permission to quit. I don't recommend waiting that long!

Once you complete your list, ask yourself, is there an action that you need to take to complete or release anything (see Day 3 of Step 2). Make a list of actions to take. Sometimes it is simply a declaration of release, such as, "I hereby release _____. It no longer serves me. I am complete." If the action takes only a few minutes, take that action. For example, it may be writing a letter or making a phone call. I realize this may feel like the hardest letter or the hardest phone call of your life. You may not have spoken with this person in years. Just do it! However, do not let this new action list stop you from releasing the issue anyway!

## CREATE A RITUAL TO LET IT ALL GO

By all, I mean everything you wrote on your first list. For example, yesterday, I bathed in a tide pool at the ocean, and the salt water washed away all that did not serve me. I cried, sang, and prayed explicitly to release everything on my list. In the end, I believed it was released; allowed myself to feel the freedom of a fresh start; and shared my gratitude with the universe for releasing the issues from me. I shredded my list afterward. You could also use your own bathtub. A friend of mine was releasing an old marriage after a divorce. She took a bath in her old wedding dress, and after lots of tears took it off in the bathtub and released the marriage energetically. (See Day 3 of Step 3 for more Spiritual Bathing ideas)

Rituals of release are essential for our minds to have completion and for the universe to assist us. That's why funerals exist. You could have a funeral for the things that no longer serve you. Honor them and bury them.

Some people like to burn their list and prefer fire to clear things away. Be careful what you ask for—another friend of mine lost her entire house in a fire.

Just declare that certain things are released and watch them fall away magically. Your declarations are often more powerful than you realize! Keep making the declaration, every day, repeatedly, until you have created a new world. Words create worlds.

Feeling overwhelmed by all the things you do? Yesterday, I released an aspect of a volunteer position that I did not enjoy. There are so many things that I enjoy doing in life, why would I spend my time doing things I don't enjoy? In this case, it made me feel important, part of a group, and I had an old story that "no one else would do it," so, like a martyr, it would have to be me, again!

This process of letting go is one of the most powerful in this entire book. Use it wisely. You do not have to carry anything that is not yours. Assume that all the adults around you are grown-ups and are responsible for their own lives, including your adult children. Codependency may make you feel needed, but it doesn't serve you or the person you are assisting to be a dependent. That doesn't mean you should suddenly dump someone for whom you have been caring. It means, you have a choice, and you can compassionately find a substitute source to care for them. That's what social services and other organizations do. You can empower the other person to be more independent. Their self-reliance will only increase the joy in your relationship. Most people don't want to be dependent on others.

What will you do with the "need" you feel to be needed? Let it go. It doesn't serve you. It is seeking validation outside of you. The answers are always within. The third step of this program is about recreating your identity, remembering who you really are, so you don't have to look outside yourself. Just being YOU is enough.

# Day 2:

Letting Go Of Attachment To Results

## AFFIRMATION:

*"I declare that I let go of any attachment I may have to the results. I choose action or non-action on its own merits."*

Now, it's time to let go of attachment to results. Don't worry, we're not letting go of our commitment to creating results in our life, but we are letting go of emotional attachment as our driving force. Instead, we are taking action because it is the "right action" regardless of the consequences. This practice is known as Satyagraha and was modeled by the life of Mahatma Gandhi[xliii], the lawyer who used non-violent action to free the country of India from England's imperialism. That's how powerful this practice can be!

From a practical perspective, imagine that the only reason you changed your eating habits was to lose weight. If you didn't lose weight in the time frame you wanted, then you would be disappointed with the results and simply quit your new program. What if instead, without attachment to whatever the scale said, you decided to eat healthy, because it was the "right action?" Then, you would continue to eat healthy regardless of the results. Had Don Quixote been attached to the results, he would have stopped fighting the windmills. In his life, it was the right action to fight windmills, so he continued to do so. I too want to be unstoppable even when things seem impossible!

A couple of steps ago, I wondered why I was still struggling with compulsive eating and old habits that I believed "should" be healed by now! When *will* I graduate, I thought. My inner wisdom said, "You will graduate when you've healed this pattern and are no longer focused on releasing addiction." Some of us may take a few weeks, some a few years, and some a few lifetimes. *It's about the quality of the transformational process, not the results.* I know that sounds crazy in a culture that rewards productivity and avoidance of suffering. I know that we judge everything by results and sometimes judge each other based on our weight or size. Release this judgment and choose a less traveled path.

Consider for a moment that you subconsciously chose addiction as something to heal in this lifetime because it was the best teacher for the spiritual lesson you wanted to learn. The sooner you learn that lesson, the sooner you can move on to the other things you are on this Earth to be and do. This lesson is not an intellectual one – it's experiential – you must actually FEEL the process and know it in your bones. If like most addicts, you avoid feeling and experiencing, then this will take a very long time. If you dive head-on into the discomfort and really give up the attachment to looking good or feeling safe, then you will fly through this. That takes a considerable amount of humility, courage, and in my case, support.

Commitment to accomplishing results is different from attachment. The attachment has an emotional component that is triggered if we don't get what we want. Emotions want to drive our decisions and our lives, especially when it comes to food choices. Making our decisions from a commitment instead of from feelings is vital. I am committed to healthy eating, regardless of how I feel. I exercise irrespective of how I feel because my ever-changing emotions do not run my life. This approach keeps us moving in the direction of our commitments regardless of how impossible it may appear.

To what are you committed? To what are you attached? Do you want to be unstoppable?

# Day 3:

. . . . . . . . . . . . . . . . . . .

## Letting Go Of Attachment To Results

### AFFIRMATION:

*"Today, I will live life to the fullest, knowing that one day, my physical body will retire and my soul will be set free."*

There's nothing better to put life in perspective than death. After my brother passed away at age thirty four, I was inspired to live life fully if only for him!

What if we always lived our life, as if we only had a few months left? One of my favorite TED Talks by a man from South America says he practices dying every Thursday.[xliv] That's the day he pretends he has been given six months to live, and he plans his bucket list. Also, every Thursday he took action on his bucket list and has now accomplished everything he set out to do. He didn't wait until he was "too old" to manifest his dreams. His method is a great model, and death is a great teacher. Have you written a bucket list yet? Set aside some time to do so. Add pictures to your vision board. Share your bucket list with others and plan to make one thing on the list happen soon!

A fun way to explore what you might like to accomplish in this lifetime is to write your own eulogy. Don't limit yourself to the things you've already accomplished, write it from the future, so you can *live into it.* Writing mine was one of the most fun exercises I've ever done! You'll see why when you read mine (see Exhibit D). It's totally crazy! I pushed the envelope for you so you can feel your own creativity expand beyond what you knew to be possible. Hope you enjoy it as much as I did.

# Day 4:

. . . . . . . . . . . . . . . . . .

## Letting go of Control

## AFFIRMATION:

*"It's not always about **me**. I give up the need to control every aspect of my life and everyone else's. All is well."*

To let go of control, you have to know what areas you are trying to control. If you're not able to see these areas clearly, just humbly ask those who know you to reveal your blind spots. Say, "Is there any aspect of my life that you see me trying to control?" If they answer, "What don't you try to control?" then pay close attention to this step and be gentle with yourself.

In my case, I like to be in control of my food. I don't want anyone to tell me what, when, or how to eat. My inner child wants everyone to get out of the way! I took the spoon from my mother's hand before I was two years old. This is a reaction to others trying to control my eating habits when I was young. I did not want others to control me, so I rebelled and decided to eat whatever I wanted, whenever I wanted, even if in secrecy. This still plays out in my life today when I sneak cold cereal for dinner.

Beyond food, I would love to be the benevolent dictator of the world and tell everyone else what to do because the arrogant part of me thinks I'd do a better job. Then I remember how much I struggle just to keep my own checkbook balanced and am grateful I don't have to balance the budget of an entire country.

Being controlling is just a symptom of fear and arrogance. However, you don't have to know why you try to control circumstances to release it. It's a choice! You simply say, "I do not need to be in control of every aspect of my life." I can accept how things are and how things are not.

Giving up control is a way of surrendering to the wisdom of my Higher Power. Whether you perceive the Divine as being within you or outside of you, or both, God's will usually works out better than our small sighted, ego-driven choices. That's why much of this program has been about getting in touch with our Divine wisdom and stepping into our mythic lives, our higher Self.

Give up the control reins to your Higher Power, and really begin to listen. What toothpaste would your Higher Power buy for you? That may sound silly, but it is a great place to start. Replace your food the same way. One by one, ask yourself, what would your higher Self-say to your little kid that wants to eat a particular food at a specific time? Maybe you start with coffee. Is the caffeine a problem for you? How is coffee working out for you? Does it make you acidic? Are you addicted? What desire is it filling? Can something else fill that void? What if you gave up control over coffee and let your Higher Power run the show? Would your life go differently?

What if, all the projects you've been waiting to start, haven't gone anywhere because you were trying to control? What if they weren't really YOURS, to begin with, and you were just intended to give the project away so that it could be accomplished in this world. What if you created leaders around you, who got all the credit for accomplishing your great ideas? What if, you were just like a hollow reed and endless ideas flowed through you? Would you get in the way trying to control the outcome? Try giving something away that feels stuck. Give it enthusiastically and with support so it can flourish.

What's the benefit of giving up control? I may actually get better results if I listen to the wisdom of real experts on food and nutrition—I don't mean the media fads. What if I let someone else create my meal plan and cook for me? I'm likely to feel better if I don't eat from rebellious reactivity. My relationships will definitely work better if I'm not judging and trying to control others. On and on goes the list. See how it feels to give up control today. Journal about giving up control.

# Day 5:

Trust The Process

## AFFIRMATION:

*"All is well. I trust the process and know that everything is in order and perfect for our spiritual development."*

I spent a whole weekend with a group of strangers for a transformational retreat once. The facilitators purposefully did not tell us the rules of the weekend so we would not know what to expect. The not knowing was unbearable for some, but instead of giving us answers to our questions, they merely responded, "Trust the process." That answer made us even more stressed out until we finally learned to relax in the unknown. That was the greatest lesson!

If the story of the past is one of betrayal and distrust, then the idea that you should just "trust the process" will be a radical and irrational departure from a safe reality scheme. Trusting an untrustworthy universe would be crazy! So, there seem to be only two options to try this on:

1. Decide to courageously choose trust in a dangerous world.

2. Rewrite your story about how the universe works.

3. The first choice takes a lot of effort and can be scary. The second approach works better and is much more efficient.

4. Let me ask you a few questions:

5. Have you survived this life so far?

6. How many years did someone feed and clothe you when you were unable to do so?

7. When you get a cut on your skin or catch a cold, does your body naturally heal or do you die?

8. After we pick the fruit off the trees, does the tree usually grow more fruit?

9. Does a seed need to be taught to grow?

10. Did this world provide you with an education of some sort?

These questions helped me realize that it's mostly the media, politics, and humanity's love for drama, that make this world feel scarier than it really is. Violence is not the norm; it's an aberration of human behavior. We spend most of our days being peaceful, but that's too boring to make history. The media loves to scare us with anything they can find—even the most recent storm. It's the same storm every year, but they sensationalize it. Statistically, the United States is safer for many groups than it's ever been.[xlv] It wasn't long ago that an African American who set foot in the State of Oregon could be killed or a Chinese American if seen above ground in Havre, Montana would be shot.

We are moving in the direction of becoming more and more loving toward each other, and the recent deluge of racist and sexist propaganda in politics is just a death rattle of an old way of life dying. The truth is that in this universe, love is the glue that holds everything together. It is our essence. I can feel this at my core. What do you feel at your core? From the bigger picture, the universe is organized, intelligent, and intentional even when it seems chaotic. This concept is often easier for those who grew up with big picture beliefs such as religion. Regardless, there is more evidence that I should trust the universe than the opposite.

Try this for even just for today. Whenever a fear or a worry pops up, just say to yourself, "Trust the process." It is your new mantra for today. See how it feels and what it opens up in your ability to do things, you would typically avoid due to fear. Courage isn't even necessary if most of the universe can be leaned into. Even black holes can be exciting adventures in the larger scheme of things. Enjoy the ride!

# Day 6:

. . . . . . . . . . . . . . . . . .

## A Kiss From The Queen Of Death

## AFFIRMATION:

*"I choose to discover what is real by releasing that which is not real."*

Will we wait for death to knock on our door before we are willing to do whatever it takes to change our lives and our eating habits? I just watched the movie "Forks over Knives,"[xlvi] and observed the success of over a dozen people who were willing to give up all animal products, refined sweeteners, and processed foods to save their lives. They all had heart disease or diabetes, and their doctor prescribed a plant-based whole foods diet to treat them. The doctor also supported their process by training them how to prepare such foods. ***The food reversed their conditions*** rather than just treating the symptom with surgery or prescriptions. This movie is an inspirational must see!

Since most humans prefer to live, avoiding death can be a great motivator for those of us who need a serious push to create new habits around our eating. This movie makes it clear that either the food we eat will help us feel great or it will kill us. For food addicts, it also numbs us out in the meantime. Why wait for a serious diagnosis to create a new you? Why wait for a loved one to go through cancer or heart attack before supporting their new diet? Just your example can save lives.

The body wants to heal itself if we could just move out of the way and give it the nutrition it really needs. It takes about 90 days to completely replace all the old blood in our circulatory system with new cells, and detoxing can allow each new blood cell you create to be totally clean. Eating whole food plants can clean our entire system from the inside out in no time! The movie, *Fat, Sick and Nearly Dead*[xlvii] also inspired me. Unlike in the film, I find that juice fasts don't provide me with enough fiber or warmth. Personally, I need warm soup to feel good and keep my inner fire lit, so I blend vegetables in my Vitamix until they're warm.

Because of my personal love affair with everything, I have also fallen in love with the Queen of Death and do not fear her kiss. Having been an estate-planning attorney and focused on the death process for almost twenty years, I am looking forward to what I call graduation day. If you're like me, it may be helpful to lean into mystical death for a meditational moment and in the process, release whatever is not real. Our minds don't know the difference between visualization and actually doing something, so let's experience death together.

Lay down comfortably where it's quiet, and you won't be disturbed for ten minutes. Cover yourself with a blanket because death can sometimes feel cold. Lower the lights and cover your face with a thin black or white veil if you have one, so you can still breathe easily. This is your death shroud. You are welcome to play the death meditation from this book's website[xlviii] If you would like to be guided through this meditation, or you can trade off reading the visualization below with a friend, or just go there yourself. Do not answer the questions out loud. Wait to speak until you return from your inner journey. The idea is that you are going to experience mystical death, without having to die physically. Notice I said "experience." This is not an intellectual exercise. Just allow yourself to go there without effort or thinking.

Close your eyes and take three deep breaths. Relax every part of your body, one by one, starting at your feet and ending at the top of your head. Feel your body feel heavier and heavier as you sink into the floor. Imagine that you have just passed away and the Queen of Death is there to greet you with a kiss. She is not scary, but a beautiful angel sent by your Higher Power to guide you to the light from which you came. She asks you to leave everything behind to make this journey.

Ask yourself these questions as you go on this journey:

♥ What must you leave behind to continue on this journey? Are you willing?

♥ What else must you leave behind to continue on this journey? (Keep asking this question until there is nothing left to leave behind).

♥ You're on the "other side" now. What do you see?

♥   How does it feel?

♥   What do you hear?

♥   Who is there with you?

♥   What do they say to you?

♥   From here, are you still able to see the world of your past?

♥   Are you able to influence it in any way?

♥   Do you want to?

♥   Did you leave anything undone?

♥   Is there anything more that needs to be known about this place?

It's time now to return to your physical body, so thank your hosts, and begin to slowly pull yourself back. Keeping your eyes closed, you start to feel your toes again, and slowly each part of your body again, working upward to your forehead. After you reach the top of your head, you gratefully wiggle your fingers and remove the veil from your face. Cupping your hands gently over your eyes, you are able to open them in the darkness without too much light. Slowly move your hands away to allow more light in. Welcome back.

Now, write in your journal about your own experience in this journey before reading any further.

Everyone has a unique experience of this journey, gleaning

whatever it is that he or she most needs to know. When I first went on this journey, I was shocked to discover that on the "other side," I was most interested in how I could help my loved ones who were still physically embodied. I noticed that my husband at the time was lonely without me, so I immediately set out to find him a girlfriend and hook him up. I wanted to ease the pain and suffering of those I had left behind.

That's when I realized that I was not alone, that many people including animals who had passed-on focused on improving the lives of those they had "left behind." The truth was we were closer to our loved ones than ever before because we were not limited by time or by the laws of the physical dimension. The hard part was that our loved ones were not aware of our presence and it was often difficult to communicate with them, but that didn't stop us. We all enjoyed the experience of "heaven," and many of us took on the role of "guardian angels."

The purpose of this exercise was to put this physical life in perspective by taking us to the end of it. It's easier to see whom we dated in high school is less important, when we are forty-seven years old looking back, although at the time it felt *really* important. Again, it presents a paradox for me—the larger perspective makes food addiction a speck of dust in the scheme of things, and it makes my victory over food addiction a crucial lesson for me. I must be willing to release everything, even my emotional attachment to food to cross over on graduation day. I thank my Higher Power, for the lessons I've learned from food addiction!

# Day 7:

Release the Illusion of Separation

## AFFIRMATION:

*"I release the illusion that I am separate from others. We are one."*

The illusion of separation may be one of the culprits in our weight gain. Imagine that some of us "put on weight" like armor to protect ourselves from others, from negative emotions, from feeling pain and from fear. The weight is real. The pain feels real, but the rest is an illusion. The stories of protection assume that everyone is separate from everyone else and that we should protect ourselves. This is not the true nature of reality unless we are in constant physical danger, such as a war zone. For most of us, it is just a story we made up, and others agreed to. What if we change the story so that we don't need protection? Are you interested in changing your story?

If you came from a Judeo-Christian background, then you already know the story of Adam and Eve in the Garden of Eden, and how their separation from God and the Garden came to be. Sinning caused them to be kicked out. Specifically, Eve took the apple from the Tree of Knowledge and Adam ate some. No more was earth like heaven, and Eve was to blame. This is a story of the separation of humanity from God, and of our punishment for it. Outside of the garden, the first two brothers were born. One killed the other, and we obviously need to protect ourselves to survive this human predicament!

Let me tell you the Hawaiian story of how humanity left the Garden of Eden as told to me by a man named Uncle Harry.[xlvii] The first human couple lived in the garden on the plateau of the crater of the volcano on the Island of Kaua'i. Everything was perfect, and they did not worry about anything. Unlike all the other plants and animals, the humans decided they wanted to discover what they did not already know, and they "chose" to leave the garden in search of the unknown. They believed they could create what did not exist and were willing to live in the unknown to do so. The other plants and animals remained in a state of bliss unaware of worry or of a desire to create. Although we share the same planet, the animals did NOT choose to leave the state-of-bliss garden with the humans.

We *chose* to leave, and for a good reason! We are discoverers who have set out on an unknown adventure. This is a much more empowering perspective not to mention fun!

Now for the twist, we never actually left the underlying reality—that we all come from the same source or that we return to that source after our body wears out. In this lifetime, we just chose to forget our innate oneness temporarily, and that we are eternal souls on a spiritual journey. The paradox is that in a small ego sense, we each have a unique personality. This makes the game of life more interesting, but in a broader spiritual sense, we are all one. That's the omnipotent reality we left to come here.

Now that you know this about yourSelf, you can let go of the illusion that there is more than just one of us here. This concept can be hard to wrap our small minds around, so just stop to feel the experience of the unity-consciousness. Have you ever felt that before? When you let it in, you will find that there is no need to protect yourself. There is no other. There is no "evil doer." You can courageously lean into the illusion of struggle rather than resist it. Struggle disappears without resistance. This approach allows me to fearlessly deal with issues head-on rather than dancing around them. From here, I have no choice but to be truthful from a place of love and connection. This view of the universe does not attack, blame or shame others because it realizes that I am also the culprit since you are just a mirror of me.

Try it with food issues—just love it to death! Adore the whole mess! Eat up your own precious humanity and laugh at the reality we have created for ourselves. It's just an adventure to discover what we don't know and to create what has never existed before. Your unique human-mind has never read this book before, so this moment is one of a kind. What will you do with the words in this book? Will you read the words and set the book on your shelf, or will you feel the words with your heart, apply them to your life and see what magic unfolds? We ARE the magic that unfolds whether we read books or not. BEING here in the inquiry, discovering and creating something new may be a story that works better for you than the old stories of your past. If you keep telling the old stories, you will get more of the past in your future! Instead, you can recreate yourself moment by moment!

This week, I decided to go by my sacred name, Vyana, because I am more Vyana than Heather now. I'm stepping more fully into my sacred life and owning my power, the power of conscious touch. Vyana is Sanscrit (over three-thousand years old) for the touch that contains one's presence or consciousness. When I touch someone, I do so consciously with love. I chose this name during a meditation on the Goddess of Compassion when I realized that holding someone in the water with full presence was the greatest gift I could give. This kind of aquatic-movement-meditation is my favorite thing to do. Imagine the magic of the warm water washing over you as your heart opens and is filled with whatever you need most while safely held in loving hands. This is bliss.

When I'm offering this kind of work in a pool of warm water, I forget time, I forget myself, I forget everything linear and find my bliss at the moment as if nothing else exists. It is the greatest natural high I've ever experienced. Do you have a hobby or something in your life that makes you feel this way? Do more of that! When you are deep in your gift and are aligned with your spiritual joy, the food will fall away as if it isn't important, except to support your calling. Other things may also fall away, such as my old name (Heather), without effort, to be replaced by the new, more authentic you. Let it go.

# STEP 13:

. . . . . . . . . . . . . . . . . .

# Spiritual Transmutation

# Day 1:

. . . . . . . . . . . . . . . . .

## Let the Magic Happen

## AFFIRMATION:

*"Just as an oyster creates a pearl from its greatest irritation, so I create pearls of wisdom."*

If you have taken, even one small step toward the healing of your body, emotionally, physically and spiritually, the universe will respond, and the magic has begun. Did you experience any breakthroughs in your relationship to food yet? You do not need to strive. This does not have to be "hard." Just your willingness is enough to prime the pump. Take a breath—we are not in a big hurry. Transmutation can happen in less than one second, or it can take whatever time it needs.

You don't have to know HOW this works any more than you need to understand how a cut on your skin heals. It just does. I've never stopped to wonder how a seed knows to grow because it just does. Instead of just trusting the process, now it's time to relax and *enjoy* the process. It's harvest time! Keep acting in alignment with the 13 Steps and begin to collect on your investment.

If you want the magic to happen faster, then focus on the 13 Steps even more, not in your head, but in your experience. Apply these 13 Steps to your life. The more seeds you plant, the larger the harvest. Choose the practices that are the most fun or the most fruitful for you.

This step is called "Spiritual Transmutation." Transformation is when your body takes on a different form. Transmutation, in contrast, is when your body actually mutates at a genetic level, and you become a different being from your core. I prefer transmutation because it suggests a deeper and more meaningful change in my essence, one that could never go back to how it was before. Have you ever heard of a butterfly becoming a caterpillar again? Exactly! You are creating a radical shift in who you are being.

You are becoming the butterfly that you were always meant to be. This is BIG, so be patient with yourself.  These 13 Steps are far more useful than simply overcoming food addiction. They can be applied to anything you desire to change or manifest. They can be applied to creating abundance, attracting your partner, or manifesting your dreams. This is just the beginning.

This process is called alchemy. Chemical alchemists once used chemistry to turn black stone into gold. Humans are not here for gold. We're here for chocolate—just kidding. We're here to be spiritual alchemists. *We are wired to transmute negative energy into positive, raising the frequency around us.* Many of us do this all the time without evening knowing it, particularly women. Our wombs seem to be the place that negative emotions congregate and are rebirthed in a positive light (often unconsciously). That's why we can end up feeling so exhausted being around negative energy. Notice if this rings true from your experience.

Crystals do the same thing. When you place two crystals next to each other. The crystal that is vibrating at the higher frequency will raise the frequency of the lower vibrating crystal.[xlviii] Guess what, humans are over 70% water! Water has a crystalline structure.

Begin to notice the magic happening all around you, inside of you, and notice how the universe is lavishing you with abundance—sometimes its abundance challenges you into a higher consciousness. It's just your job to **notice, receive and be grateful.** That may be a new muscle for you. It may take some effort to stop and notice this new way of being in a universe, which is conspiring to support you.

Now that you have released the old (Step 12), you are totally free to embrace **the new.** Your life is a blank canvas on which you may create what has never been before! Your unique visions and soul longings are waiting to be born, often from within the contrast of your sufferings.

Only YOU can bring this unique form of beauty to the world. Only you can be the alchemist of that particular offering. Do not waste time, if the seed is blooming, get any limiting thoughts out of the way, and allow miracles to show up! Your job is to help water the dream, add good food and some sunshine both physically and metaphorically.

# Day 2:

· · · · · · · · · · · · · · · · · ·

## Eating For Spiritual Transmutation

## AFFIRMATION:

*"Food is my medicine. I choose food that supports and transforms my body, mind, and spirit for its highest purpose."*

Fasting and feasting are both used for spiritual enlightenment. Both are a divine gift depending on what you need at the moment. One is for clearing, and one is for celebration. Although I encourage you to enjoy both, this 13th Step is the victory and feasting is in order! Let's use delicious, healthy food to celebrate your victory instead of food that no longer serves you! If you don't feel victorious now, let's pretend you are. Fake it 'till you make it. Just act sober if you have to.

Let's make one of your meals today a sensory feast! Choose each item of food based on two criteria: 1) Does it support your health, and 2) Does it taste delicious? Make a platter—not just a plate—and place your food items on it in a way that feels like beautiful art. Take a picture of your feast. You do not have to be the one to prepare it, but you must participate at least by mindfully eating some of it.[23]

Mindful eating means focusing your attention ONLY on the experience of the food. That means no talking! Experience the smell of the food before you place it in your mouth. How does it feel on your lips? How does it look? Chew it until you can't chew it anymore. All life forms have a vibration and a color frequency. Can you feel the life force of the food or has the food been cooked so much that it no longer exists? What is the texture like? Of what does it remind you? Rate it from 1 to 10. Does it taste different if you bless it first? Does it taste different if you create an intention like, "As I eat this water-melon, my body is healed by its sweetness"? What if:

- ♥ You add beautiful music to the experience or set the table to honor your feast.

- ♥ You light a candle or two for your table.

- ♥ You eat while taking a bath.

- ♥ You eat in the garden tonight at sunset.

- ♥ You invite others to join you.

- ♥ You ask them to bring some food that meets your criteria.

Your love for food can be a beautiful thing, it is not something to avoid.

---

[23] *If you were raised to eat everything on your plate, I recommend releasing that old habit. If you were raised not to waste food, you have permission for this feast to be free of that expectation.*

The purpose of this exercise is:

1.  To remind us that it IS possible to find foods that are both delicious and good for our bodies.

2.  To remind us that when we mindfully eat, we experience our food in a more fulfilling way, and probably need less than we think.

3.  To remind us that whatever we intend our food to be, it can become.

4.  To remind us that it is wonderful to celebrate ourselves, even with food.

Remembering that my food can become what I intend it to be is tremendously helpful when I'm offered food that does not fit my food plan. I can simply wave my magic wand and transmute the food! We all have the power to change anything with prayer and intention. Here's a quote from a wise mermaid,

"You can call it stale crackers and cheap wine, or you can call it Holy Communion. Intention is EVERYTHING."

Even the monks who beg for food and eat from trash cans in India receive everything they need from it. They gratefully transform their food into nourishment. Why do you think so many cultures pray over their food before they eat it? I highly recommend it!

Keep Calm and Feast On!

# Day 3:

Enrolling Others in Your Vision

## AFFIRMATION:

*"I love to provide others with the opportunity to support my dreams and contribute to them."*

I walked into a coffee shop recently, and a stranger smiled and said, "Oh you're the mermaid lady. You're funny!" That was just what I needed to hear. The conversation reminded me of my mythic-self and one of the gifts I bring. Perfect!

Recently, by offering comedy at the open mic while dressed as my mersona, I had enrolled others in supporting my reality. Enrolling others in your transmutation process is critical to supporting your long-term success. When others see you as the magnificent being that you are, then they will remind you if, and when, you forget. This creates a conspiracy—a good one!

Our job is three-fold:

1. To translate our mission clearly so others can get it.

2. To understand others, so that we can share "what's in it for them."

3. To enroll others in the project.

For this exercise, first, you must decide in what part of your life you desire to enroll others. Where do you want more support? Recently, I chose to enroll others in my exercise plan because that is where I needed the most support. I created a three-step approach:

1. **TRANSLATE THE MISSION.** I desire to exercise at least once every day for 45 minutes. I prefer to be outside in the sunshine, ideally in the water, and having fun.

2. **DECIDE WHO IS NEEDED AND WHAT'S IN IT FOR THEM.** In this case, I enrolled my spouse in supporting me in this project. What's in it for him is a healthy, happy partner who feels great and wants to contribute back to our relationship. This step means that you must know your audience and know what makes them passionate about something. You have to understand what makes them tick and what makes them motivated to help.

3. **EXPLAIN THE SUPPORT NEEDED.** I explained to my spouse that I needed the morning time to exercise, especially for swimming and reminded him what was in it for him. I asked him what he thought he could do to help me. He immediately offered to take over preparing breakfasts for our eight to ten guests each morning here at the Bed & Breakfast so

that I could exercise. Wow! That was more than I expected and felt wonderful!

Now, you can move onto the next enrollment conversation. Maybe it's help with a food plan, or getting childcare, so you have time for spiritual deepening.

I love to enroll others in the identity that I'm creating as a mermaid and in all the creative projects that I imagine. There are so many wonderful ideas in the world that need leadership, and I can't do them all by myself. It is my job to enroll others, and not just once, but *again and again* to keep them enrolled in the excitement of "what's in it for them."

You are creating leaders around you. It's a gift to them, to you and the world. Therefore, it's not enough to enroll my spouse in cooking breakfast every morning for the rest of his life. I need to share my appreciation for his contribution so that he will feel how much it means to me, and as he sees the results of my exercise, he'll continue to enroll in my plan.

This works well for creative ideas as well. Don't keep them to yourself share them. You would be surprised how your vision(s) may inspire many others to contribute. Be specific with people about what you need. In addition to one-on-one conversations, many wonderful websites nowadays can help you such as "GoFundMe.com" or "Kickstarter.com" or "Indegogo.com," for example. Make a list of all the creative ideas you've dreamed of completing but haven't. What stops you? I'm guessing it's support. Maybe you're only a few enrollment conversations away from putting the support you need in place.

# Day 4:

. . . . . . . . . . . . . . . . . .

## Expect Miracles

## AFFIRMATION:

*"Every day in every way, I'm getting happier and happier, healthier and healthier, more and more alive, radiant and self-expressed! I live a miraculous life."*

Sometimes the universe surprises us with miracles. When was the last time you experienced a miracle? When was the last time you stopped to notice a miracle happening around you? When you step into your mythic, magical, gigantic higher self, miracles begin to happen more and more often because you are in greater alignment with Divine will. Get used to it.

Miraculous healings can happen whether you believe or not. A few months ago, one of my guests wanted to visit a shaman about pain in her back. The Shaman was booked up, so I sent her to the Farmer's Market where a particular massage therapist could offer some help. When she arrived at the market, she noticed an older man blowing a conch shell for no apparent reason. She watched him curiously, and he reached out to touch a stranger walking by. The stranger turned toward the man immediately and her facial expressions suggested that she had just experienced a significant spontaneous healing. The woman was speechless.

My guest kept making eye contact with the older man who appeared to be at the market for no apparent reason. She finally approached him and explained to him about her back. He suggested she see a doctor. However, the older man gently touched the guest's boyfriend who had not shared his health concern with anyone nor had he requested help. The guest's boyfriend experienced a spontaneously healing of significance. Not a believer in such things, he walked the garden for hours in tears, not knowing how to hold this new possibility. It completely changed his health and his perception of the universe.

While it's not necessary to believe in miracles to experience them, I've noticed that people who are open to miracles are more likely to attract them, notice them and to perform them. Being open-minded to the possibility of miracles primes the pump. Actively requesting miracles or creating your own really gets the ball rolling.

For example, the next time you have a food craving and feel like your white knuckling it, just ask for a miracle! Then stop and notice what the miracle may be, and be sure to be grateful for it. My miracle last week was watching an inspirational movie that completely lifted my spirit and made it easy to eat healthy this week – even my husband is inspired. Sometimes my miracle happens during a massage or a conversation when synchronicities align. I usually get the chills, and everything falls into place in the face of a miracle.

YOU are a miracle if you think about it. Science still cannot explain how YOU came to be the way you are with all your billion, billion, billions of atoms connecting to each other in a particular way. You are unique in the world, and no one can replicate you. Even cloning doesn't capture your personality or soul. No one knows your inner workings. You don't even have to think about breathing, it's just automatic—pretty cool!

Miracles are all around us. Each flower you see is a miracle, showing up at this particular moment to say hello to you. Each person you meet is a miracle, and it's your job to figure out why. Each piece of food that reaches your lips is a miracle. Think about where it came from, who created it, and how many trucks had to bring it to your grocery store to make it to your plate.

Miraculous healings are available to all of us. I believe that those who perform healing miracles see the one in need of healing as a whole and complete, because the soul cannot be sick, diseased or addicted. Healers see through the illusion. They are able to remember us in our perfection, not through the filter of our symptoms created by a story of "something is wrong." That means we can all be "healers" if we are willing to remember each other as perfect. Try seeing yourself this way. Try seeing everyone else as perfect rather than seeing what's wrong.

Keep a miracle journal next to your bed and ask yourself what miracles you either received, witnessed or created that day. This will keep miracles top of mind, even in your Dreamtime. This will also help fill up your gratitude journal.

haven't. What stops you? I'm guessing it's support. Maybe you're only a few enrollment conversations away from putting the support you need in place.

# Day 5:

. . . . . . . . . . . . . . . . . .

## Claiming Ecstasy

## AFFIRMATION:

*"I am free to choose ecstasy under all circumstances."*

When you have the ***freedom to choose*** how you interpret what happens to you in life, then you are free to choose ecstasy under all circumstances. My fairy godmother says,

> *"Ecstasy is perceiving the Divine order in all occurrences, no exceptions."*[xlix]

If we trust the Divine order, then we can feel the ecstasy of being part of that Divine order, in whatever role we happen to be playing.

We need not choose to suffer as our path to enlightenment. We are free to choose joy, love and even pleasure, instead. These are always available to us, but sometimes we are blind to that choice. Even if we know we have a choice, we don't often practice choosing a different feeling, one that feels better than the one before. Just reach for a better feeling, and eventually, you'll get to ecstasy. We can generate our feelings regardless of our circumstances:

♥   You can choose to feel sad, angry, frustrated, and upset.

♥   You can choose to feel numb, checked-out, and stoic.

♥   You can choose to feel acceptance, compassion, and kindness.

♥   You can choose to feel love, joy, and ecstasy!

This is true freedom when you are the master of your emotions rather than your emotions running your life like a roller coaster.

You will attract emotions that are more ecstatic if you choose to generate them, and you will create a life of ecstasy. Go where you are invited. Follow your heart and your bliss. Live your dreams! You always have a choice.

It's easy to feel ecstatic when things are going well, but even our challenges can be ecstatic when we see them through a certain lens. By choosing this human life, for example, we have invited the entire universe to initiate us in the art of being a huge soul stuffed inside a very small physical body.

Maybe we're here to see just how deep our love can go even in the face of war, injustice, chaos, and corruption.

Maybe we weren't spiritually evolved enough to pass such a test before, and the universe keeps increasing the strength of the test to help us expand even more. It was an extreme test that Jesus passed when he was crucified, and his dying words were prayers of forgiveness on the executioner's behalf. He transformed a horrific experience into a spiritual victory that would be remembered by humanity for thousands of years. If even physical death can become ecstatic within its spiritual context, is there anything that we cannot transform?

Take the conversation about transgender bathrooms for example. Our brains love to feel safe by creating little boxes to categorize things so we can pretend we understand them, particularly around topics like sexuality. Gender is one such construct, and most of us cling to it as if it's our identity. On the continuum of male and female, we have words for the extremes and for a few places in the middle—ultra male, butch, fem, gay, bisexual, lesbian, flaming, for example. What we don't realize is that these boxes and labels are limiting given that we all carry male and female qualities. These are part of our self-expression when others allow us to be more than just one label. These constructs do not just limit our sexuality they limit our potential. The only reason gender matters so much are because one gender (the masculine) still dominates, and so it is less valuable to many societies to identify as female. It's mostly just a power construct designed to oppress half of the population. Gender suppression in India means that most girls who live in villages, for example, still carry water, and therefore have no time to attend school. It seems funny to me now that we give so much meaning to whatever genitalia we happen to be born with.

Most of us don't realize that we are all "transgender" to some extent on the gender continuum. Therefore, the gender conversation is just an opportunity to love more deeply those who appear to be different and to allow ourselves more freedom to move around on the continuum.

It is also an opportunity, if we're not afraid of perceived differences, to celebrate diversity. In the last 50 years, we danced around the issue of race, and now we are evolving to appreciate diversity more and more. Before that, the issue was religion and resulted in learning tolerance for those who do not go to the same church, synagogue or mosque. We are shaking these old prejudices now. They are no longer the norm in the United States, and we are no longer silent about these issues.

What if instead of feeling stress around issues of gender, race, and religion, we enjoyed the adventure of learning more about each other and ourselves. I love learning things I didn't know before, and experiencing other cultures exposes me to thinking that is outside my own cultural norm. I've always thought it would be exciting to meet extra-terrestrials so I could learn from them. I don't have to go far to have that same imagined experience with the vast diversity of the human family! That's exciting to me. That's one reason I love to live in Hawai'i. I was raised in a different culture. Hawaii expands how I experience things. I'm curious about what humans don't know and of what we are still unaware.

Spend today being curious about everyone. Ask many questions. With no fear, enjoy the human diversity around you that may be hiding because of judgmental attitudes. Let others show their colors to you. When you see the flowers in full bloom in this garden of humanity, beauty will shine, and joy will be the result. Cultivate such a garden in your own life. Let yourself be happy under all circumstances and let your ecstasy be seen.

# Day 6:

. . . . . . . . . . . . . . . . . .

## The Power of Soul Stories

## AFFIRMATION:

*"The story of my soul is vast, without beginning or end, without limits at all."*

One of my most ecstatic moments in life was having dinner with my Faerie Godmother, Ariel Spilsbury[i], a few years ago. We decided we wanted to have a mythic dinner, just the two of us. We would each come in a mythic persona, which we did not reveal until we met at the restaurant. The restaurant we chose was the Panama Hotel in San Rafael, California, a quaint bed & breakfast where the service and food are heartfelt. She came as her magical Fairy Godmother Self with flowing gown, tiara and magic bag. I came as a "magical moment collector" in a hot pink, black, and white Punjabi with a matching veil over a small top hat. She was there to create magic, and I was there to collect the moments. Perfect!

The other guests in the intimate restaurant setting noticed how much fun we were having with our mythic conversations and clear adoration for each other. The table of four next to us finally dared to ask if we were celebrating something. We said, "Oh yes, we're collecting magical moments. Would you like to collect a magical moment with us?" They responded, "Yes." We explained that the next time a magical moment was about to happen, we would let them know.

About two minutes later, a radiant woman walks across the restaurant directly toward me and says, "I have a gift for you." This is not an unusual circumstance in the mythic realm, so I was not too surprised by a total stranger approaching me with gifts. I was delighted, and we invited the table of four next to us to join in. They all stood and held hands in a semi-circle around our little table while the beautiful stranger began to sing an ancient Sufi poem by Hafiz. It sounded like a melodious chant from an ancient world, but completely spontaneous at the same time, as though no one had sung this melody before. The entire restaurant was silent to hear the exquisite offering. It was like nothing I had ever heard before and something that felt like home at the same time. The four people from the table next to us were speechless by the magical gift and sat down again at their own table, at which time, my Faerie God-mother, pulled a scroll from her magic bag, the exact same poem by Hafiz that the singer had just transmitted as a gift. Now, I had the poem in writing. Significantly, the poem was about a bird that had flown out of a dark cave to find its beloved in the sunlight. It would never return to its cave as it had found its beloved (the Divine) and sat on the rim of a crystal chalice. Spiritually, this is how I felt when I emerged from sitting behind a desk after 20 years practicing law within the constraints of an archaic system and discovered myself in the water offering mermaid meditation-and-movement sessions. Finally, I had total freedom to fly.

Synchronistically, my Faerie Godmother opened her magic bag one more time and bestowed a crystal chalice upon me with a bird on it. Wow! However—wait—that's not all! The mysterious singer observed in silence this gift exchange and then said to me, "I have another gift for you." Now, I was really blown away. I already was lavished with gifts beyond my wildest imagination, and yet there's MORE? She said that we needed more privacy and she took my hand and led me to the foyer of the restaurant where we sat holding hands. She explained that she had come to tell my soul story. I did not know what a soul story was and I was intrigued. She closed her eyes for about 30 seconds, giggled and shared a metaphorical vision that I will never forget! It included a flying giraffe, a pink pillbox hat, playful adventure through the universe, and a star in my heart that lights the path so others can find me. It also included rest.

This story was very different from the serious lawyer that I have played out for two decades at the expense of my health and happiness. I have spent most of my life feeling the need to end suffering in the world, to fight injustice, and wanting to remedy human rights abuses. The way that I held this cause felt overwhelming and urgent. That's why I went to law school in the first place. How could I possibly play or enjoy abundance when human lives were at stake? I felt the weight of the world on my shoulders since about age three.

To hear the giraffe story of how I may have landed on this planet so playfully, so effortlessly, made me feel like a cosmic adventurer, here for a short time, to enjoy the friends that will find me through the light that shines from my heart.

This new story gave me permission to relax and enjoy the ride.

This playful tale where there was no mention of my responsibility to save humanity from its suffering set me free. I could just hold the light and let those who were drawn by it find me. Having been an overachiever my entire life, to think that it could feel effortless and the entire universe would conspire with me was a radical shift. The story we tell ourselves about how we came to be and why we are here sets the stage or the context for the rest of our lives.

I've carried this story with me in my move to Hawai'i, where I am giving myself permission to rest for the first time in my life. I know that as I shine my light out from my retreat center, I am a magnet for those who are meant to visit me here. This oasis of beauty and peace nourishes my soul. The Aloha of the island inspires my love. The manna (power) of the sacred places of forgiveness here is washing away all that does not serve me and preparing me to receive others with an open heart. May we all be magic moment collectors! What is your soul story?

# Day 7:

· · · · · · · · · · · · · · · · ·

## Completion

AFFIRMATION:

*"I declare that I am complete, healed and do not need food or a certain kind of body to feel emotionally fulfilled."*

# Congratulations

**You have now completed the *13 Steps to Freedom From Food Addiction!* Say the above affirmation aloud.**

If you are currently binging and reading this book at the same time, don't be ashamed, just put down the Twinkie first, so the statement is true at this moment. When I first completed these steps, I hadn't lost any weight yet. Then 30 pounds dropped off my body in just a few weeks. I went from a size twelve to a six without effort, just working the steps.

Continue to make this affirmation statement and continue to apply these steps. Continue to heal, layer by layer in a spiraling fashion; "fake it till you make it," until the gaps between our weak spots widen; and you can *confidently* declare the truth of this statement. You are not alone, and you can start over at every moment. As they say in AA, Alcoholics Anonymous, "One day at a time."

Aren't you glad this isn't a boot camp and that you are not a perfectionist! I am so grateful for gentleness, kindness, and honesty in this program.

You are probably wondering what's next. Now it's time to contribute to others, and not only for altruistic reasons. By supporting someone else's recovery, you will strengthen your own. You may not need a support group now, but they need you! We all love to make a difference in the lives of others. Now it's your turn to give back or pay it forward, whatever works for you.

Meaning and purpose, which is where happiness is most easily accessed, come from our ability to contribute to others. They will keep you coming back week after week. Your practicing the program will inspire others, and their lives will change because of your example. You cannot contribute if you feel like you have nothing to give. You have been given a gift, now you can *help others heal* in the future. That's right this program doesn't end after you alone are healed. This is not a one-way relationship. Contributing to others is the price we pay for the privilege of being on this beautiful planet.

The good news is that you don't have to be perfect to help others. In fact, in my experience, the more real you are, the better. If I had waited for perfection to write this book, it would never have been written. If you have read and applied most of these steps to your life, then you are ready to help others on their path to recovery from food addiction. Begin by joining a support group that is working these 13 Steps and be a buddy to someone. Reach out. Give generously. Be an example of what freedom and victory look like.

You may even decide you want to facilitate support groups. To apply for the certification program, go to one of my sites:

**www.DivingIntoTheDivineFeminine.com**

# You did it!

Keep up the great work and put yourself out there for others!

## About

# VYANA REYNOLDS

After spending a year in Istanbul, Turkey, at age nineteen, Vyana went to law school to make a difference in the lives of women and girls internationally, focusing on human rights. She drafted and successfully lobbied the passage of Federal Legislation to assist people with disabilities in 1997. For her pro bono projects at the nation's capital, she received the Excellence for the Future Award, Center for Applied Legal Instruction, the 1997 National Pro Bono Publico Award, and the Pro Bono Students of America. She also received the Equal Justice Foundation Fellowship Grant and the Public Interest Award from Georgetown University Law Center and graduated with honors. After a little over a year of civil rights trial work in Oakland, California, she founded her own law firm focusing solely on estate planning. The legal world valued her intelligence and strong work ethic, leaving most of her other innate gifts still untapped.

Sixteen years later, Vyana was able to bridge the duality of living a mythic life in the "real" world by selling her law practice and moving to Kona, Hawai'i, to open Mermaid Dreams Bed and Breakfast. She explores her femininity through the mythical mermaid experience. The mythic play reveals her greatest gifts. The name Vyana is Sanskrit for "conscious touch." She offers aquatic meditative movement, mythic makeovers, sacred bathing, ancient anointing with essential oils, as well as mermaid coaching. She obtained her training from the 13 Moon Mystery School, the Emerald Temple, Harbin School of Healing Arts, and is currently apprenticing with Aquamystica in Ashland, Oregon. She has been blessed with a family lineage of healing arts including Rolfing, Osteopathy, Naturopathy, Acupuncture, and Homeopathy. She honors all religions and mystical traditions in her work.

Born in Tacoma, Washington, Vyana spent her childhood fishing on the cold waters of Puget Sound, curious about what could possibly live in the darkness 300 feet below the surface. Vyana also stands for clean and healthy oceans. She founded the Kona Mermaid School and the Mermaid Ambassador Program as a way to help others fall in love with the oceans again, to be ambassadors of the ocean and to discover their gifts through mythic play as mermaids. She is currently involved with the Education Committee of the Hawai'i Dolphin Initiative on the Big Island of Hawai'i.

# EXHIBIT A

## A Few Possibilities You May Choose to Generate

| | | |
|---|---|---|
| Wisdom | Health | Sexiness |
| Power | Consciousness | Vibrancy |
| Greatness | Beauty | Lightness |
| Abundance | Disciplined | Balance |
| Creativity | Magic | Harmony |
| Inspiration | Worthiness | Contribution |
| Wealth | Softness | Happiness |
| Strong | Authenticity | Healing |
| Joy | Nurturance | Empowering |
| Peace | Trust | Passion |
| Love | Wholeness | Fun |
| Kindness | Delight | Compassion |
| Forgiveness | Freedom | Curiosity |
| Gentleness | Deliciousness | Acceptance |
| Opulence | Excitement | Flexibility |
| Integrity | Adventure | Stewardship |
| Impeccability | Connection | Service |
| Generosity | Adoration | Bliss |
| Responsibility | Ecstasy | Discernment |
| Courage | Open-heartedness | Grace |
| Vitality | Pleasure | |

# EXHIBIT

## My Theme Song

I converted the disempowering song called "In my life" from Les Miserable to one of victory, but I kept the epic tune. Here are my new lyrics:

*In my heart, I am holding a star that emblazons a pathway of light.*
*In that path, there is so much abundance and beauty*
*and carefree delight.*
*How is this? My life so incredibly blessed.*
*I reach for the stars. They reach back and say, "Yes!"*

*I even know what it means to be me.*
*My purpose is clear, and I'm totally free.*
*I'm here fulfilling the dream in me.*

*Take a ride on my carpet of magic. Believe me, it flies all the time.*
*Come along. See all creation as ours like a beautiful song.*
*Make it up. That's what we do anyway.*
*Have no fear, let's jump in all the way!*

*I am here to be love. I am here to be real.*
*Deep down in my heart, I can feel what you feel.*
*Here to remember the gifts we bring.*

# EXHIBIT

## My Sacred Trust

I, Vyana Reynolds, a resident of Planet Earth in the Milky Way Galaxy, declare that I hold certain realities in trust, to be held, administered and distributed according to the following terms:

- ♥ I declare all beings who choose to be, cancer-free and disease-free.

- ♥ I declare emotional intimacy for all beings.

- ♥ I declare a world of poetry, mysticism and of subtle beauty and ecstasy.

- ♥ I declare expansive and unconditional love even in the midst of the appearance of contraction.

- ♥ I declare all beings free to fulfill our greatest authentic potential and Self-expression.

- ♥ I declare all waterways rich with diversity and healthy for the inhabitants.

- ♥ I declare spiritual and religious freedom for all.

- ♥ I declare all beings sober from addiction.

- ♥ I declare a symbiotic human relationship with our planet.

- ♥ I declare connection, love, and laughter as the norm.

- ♥ I declare education that inspires virtues, intelligence (emotional too), curiosity and freedom to cultivate an open mind.

- ♥ I declare the mind as a tool in service to the heart.

- ♥ I declare that life is revered with awe and wonder.

- ♥ I declare a planet where individuals feel part of a community, with nature and the cosmos in such a way that their behavior considers and contributes to others.

- ♥ I declare a planet in which diverse discourse is respected, and everyone feels heard.

- ♥ I declare a world in which natural disasters are anticipated in advance and therefore create minimal damage to living beings.

- ♥ I declare compassion for all beings as though we are in the process of spiritual development, individually and as one humanity.

- ♥ I declare 100% responsibility for the world we create.

- ♥ I declare no victims or perpetrators, only opportunities for resilience, clarity through contrast, the victory of spirit, courage, empathy, and forgiveness.

- I declare deep listening to adversity as a great teacher. Vibrant health and vitality are the norms. Healing is easily understood and easily accessible.

- I declare "hard work" ethic replaced by the playful contribution of our gifts.

- I declare joy in remembrance of each other's gifts and talents.

- I declare effortless telepathic communication with animals of all species.

- I declare access to safe contraception and reproductive choices for all beings who can make that choice. I declare that they make that choice from the abundance of resources and support.

- I declare clean drinking water for the planet.

- I declare freedom from the pollution of all kinds.

- I declare interdimensional awareness such that we can communicate with other realms and mythic beings such as angels and the fairies.

- I declare that all humans are free to express their gender(s).

- I declare peace and abundance such that all beings can focus on their spiritual and artistic gifts and that love-centered mystery schools exist to help us remember them.

♥   I declare that this Sacred Trust will become a movement
    to which others will add their truths, and we will stand
    together and find strength in each other's vision for the
    future.

♥   I declare that I have read the preceding declaration of Trust.
    I approve this declaration in all particulars and agree to be
    bound by its terms and conditions.

*Dated: April 4, 2016, Mermaid Vyana*

# EXHIBIT

## Eulogy for Vyana

Many of you knew her as Heather Reynolds. This mystical mermaid was also known as Vyana. She was one of the greatest philanthropists Earth has ever known.

What most never knew was that she was a steward of the Milky Way Galaxy. In her Dreamtime, she would meet with the galactic counsels and negotiate the spread of useful new technologies for this planet. She was a master of diplomacy, particularly across species, where she could transmute fear into laughter and trust at light speed. She would acquire new technologies and then inspire inventors to create them here on Earth to assist humanity. Giving away ideas, creating leaders, and supporting their success behind the scenes were her favorite pastimes.

Her wealth of mystical metaphor, mastery of humor, vast collection of magical moments and creative eruptions were highly sought after, and she traded them for the newest technology. One such trade was the bubble field. Some of you remember when we used to live in dense square boxes made of wood and sheetrock. Now we just say the word "bubble" to our smartphones and have a protective floating shelter on demand. This lightweight iridescent force field provides sanctuary wherever we may be, even floats on water. Similarly, since the invention of "the manifesto machine," we don't need to hoard food, water or clothing—we just manifest what we need when we need it, seemingly out of thin air.

This ability came from the revolutionary idea that the third dimension reality is a focused vibration that creates density. The machine assists our minds to focus long enough to attract a parallel vibration, which appears in our space at the appointed time. This invention finally freed humanity from its long history of slavery, sometimes cloaked as employment. Now all humans can meet their needs without over-consuming the planet, so they focus now on their artistic abilities, spiritual gifts, and quality relationships.

Vyana was an explorer. Her adventures took her to the depths of the ocean where she was given maps of each underwater eco-village—and the light of these maps shined out across the water at night to illumine the beauty way (as opposed to valuing the most efficient way—a theme when scarcity ruled). The creatures of the sea can feel these maps for navigation purposes and know the way even in changing circumstances such as polar melt. In ancient times, we would navigate by the stars, now we can navigate by heart—and I don't just mean the oceans.

She wasn't always fearless in her travels, but her courage always triumphed, and the victory of her spirit was rewarded. Her favorite place on earth was about eighty feet under water in the Puget Sound, where it's so dark you can't tell which way is up anymore, except that the undersea garden of sea plumes are glowing so iridescent that they light up the entire sea floor like a symphony of white flowering lights.

I'll never forget when from Dreamtime, she brought back the remembrance of vibrational technology to psychically heal ourselves, each other and end disease for all creatures unless consciously chosen. She could start the healing process by merely asking the right question – not just a superficial question, but the core question. Usually something simple like "And what does your pain want to say right now?"

The gold standard was replaced in her lifetime by humor, emotional intimacy, and chocolate, her personal favorites, which attracted her to Earth in the first place.

The merfolk of the world democratically elected Vyana to be an Ambassador of the Sea and to speak on their behalf to humanity. She only remembered how to shapeshift into her dolphin tale toward the latter half of her life – a skill that most of us had forgotten at the time. Were it not for her pure-hearted, vulnerable willingness to take certain leaps into joy—regardless of how dire the circumstances seemed at the turn of the last century—the vibration of the planet might not have flown off the charts. This attracted the technology necessary to clean the Earth's oceans, the air, and the soil. Earth was given a deep clean by the use of seaweed, mushroom, and fungal kingdoms. The symbiotic existence of humans and the planet was restored. The entire mermaid movement continues to this day to maintain this harmonious balance.

In gratitude, Vyana was rewarded with an underwater home of her design, lit by phytoplankton and sound bubbles (star in a jar technology). The spherical shapes of the spaces removed any concern of pressure, and now humans can live underwater just as easily as above. The design is driven by PLAY – a wisdom teaching of the dolphin community in which Vyana had attained a "black belt."

The best part is that humanity has been humbled by the generosity of the universe and humans have remembered their nobility again. There is a knowing of their worthiness and from that a natural gratitude for the awe and wonder of this creation.

When Vyana was born, diversity was dying out, and creatures were becoming extinct, but now the planet is becoming more and more diverse as creatures begin to choose their mutations more consciously.

The radiant beauty that she saw in all beings, she shared freely. Her life was a love affair with everything. Vyana lived up to her name—she consciously touched everything with love, and miracles happened. She saw and felt the light vibration of all she met, and reminded them of their greatest gifts, inspiring them to share— delighting the entire universe. Each moment she collected in this lifetime was magical because she made it so.

She solved the scarcity epidemic of the last 6 thousand years by declaring prosperity instead. This new reality caught on and soon became the norm.

All the earth's prior concerns were eradicated soon after she launched the Sacred Trust campaign where everyone declared reality together—to see how much of their visions overlapped and to realize how much psychic energy they could focus on creating heaven on earth.

Vyana's visionary ideas were never actually hers—they belonged to the collective. However, when she spoke them, they were implemented across the galaxy and have brought peace, connection, collaboration and prosperity to many planets. She is most known for her bubble theory of Self and the Spiral Time Hypothesis. The latter moved us away from thinking of time as linear (which felt limiting), to a way of thinking more like a Mobius strip between dimensions, never-ending, always just the other side of the same veil—so close you can reach through to the other side. Time follows the same golden mean spiral as everything else. This approach blew the roof off every mathematical equation, and quantum physics exploded with new possibilities.

Vyana's commitment, as a peacemaker, to speaking truth from compassion paved the way for clarity and avoided unnecessary suffering.

Vyana chose this pivotal moment on earth to assist in midwifing humanity beyond its limited thought forms to its greatest potential. She was instrumental in inspiring pure-hearted beings to identify and use their gifts such as the healing arts, clairvoyant archaeology, and underwater architecture with a focus on water and light. I'll never forget the first day she had a levitational tea party – everyone giggled in delight as he or she floated about drinking a favorite tea.

She appeared for a time here as a seemingly separate entity from you—but she would want me to remind you that it's just an illusion—her essence is closer to you now than ever before electrically speaking. As such, she will continue to cheer you on behind the scenes to fulfill YOUR dreams!

# EXHIBIT

## My Purpose

I am a fountain of love and a creator of beauty on an adventure to discover our gifts and enjoy prosperity.

## AFFIRMATIONS:

- ♥ I am committed to creating fulfilling relationships.

- ♥ I own, cultivate and share my many gifts and talents.

- ♥ I choose vitality and well-being in every moment.

- ♥ I choose my beliefs and how they make me feel. I am free.

- ♥ I am happy and healthy inside and out.

- ♥ I love and accept myself just the way I am, unconditionally.

- ♥ I am pure joy and a magnet for fun!

- ♥ I celebrate my success and create a life I love.

- ♥ I am more and more authentic every day as I discover and create mySelf.

- ♥ I am a beautiful temple within my body for my magnificent soul.

- ♥ I have a brilliant mind.

- ♥ I have energy which is pure delight and ripples out to the world.

- ♥ I am discerning about the character of others and choose to relate to people who are good for me.

- ♥ I create a life which is by invitation only. I create and choose everything in my life.

- ♥ I take time every day to nurture myself.

- ♥ I develop myself every day in every way.

- ♥ I am deeply connected to others and myself.

- ♥ I am open-minded and open-hearted.

- ♥ I am open to sharing intimacy and vulnerability.

- ♥ I notice and appreciate the beauty in and around us every day.

# EXHIBIT

## Treat Ideas for Heather

♥ Get a massage.

♥ Have a hot bath.

♥ Turn on the music and dance around the house.

♥ Watch a good movie or comedy and laugh.

♥ Create a tea party for friends.

♥ Make a gift for someone in the art room.

♥ Ask my sweetie for a foot rub or play with my hair.

♥ Go swimming.

♥ Make a funny movie with my iPhone.

♥ Have a game night with friends.

♥ Plan my next birthday.

♥ Create art.

♥ Clean and reorganize a closet or drawer just for fun.

- ♥ Update my bucket list by looking at adventures online.

- ♥ Plan my next vacation adventure.

- ♥ Drop into meditation to find my joy.

- ♥ Work in the garden, listen to the birds and admire the flowers.

# EXHIBIT

## *G*

## Vitality Chart

|  | Mon. | Tues. | Wed. |
|---|---|---|---|
| SPIRITUAL TIME |  |  |  |
| SLEEP |  |  |  |
| VITAMINS |  |  |  |
| HEALTHY FOOD |  |  |  |
| WATER |  |  |  |
| PLAY VS. STRESS |  |  |  |
| DEEP |  |  |  |
| BREATHING |  |  |  |
| BONUS FOR MASSAGE ETC. |  |  |  |
| HOW I FEEL? |  |  |  |

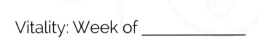

Vitality: Week of _____

| Thur. | Fri. | Sat. | Sun. |
|-------|------|------|------|
|       |      |      |      |
|       |      |      |      |
|       |      |      |      |
|       |      |      |      |
|       |      |      |      |
|       |      |      |      |
|       |      |      |      |
|       |      |      |      |
|       |      |      |      |
|       |      |      |      |

# EXHIBIT

## My Journal Entry—a Dance with Depression

Today I realized that depression and anxiety have little to do with reality or my current circumstances, and I have been reaching for something to make me feel better—food, movies, shopping, etc.—rather than admit that I'm anxious and depressed.

I only realized this today because *I stopped long enough to feel.* This was the same feeling I had when I was a stressed-out lawyer, over a year ago. Today, I'm living the dream in Hawaii! How could this possibly be?

I'm ashamed of my state of mind because I think I should know better. I assume that my life choices have something to do with this state of mind and it must reflect a lack discipline. My head says, "If only I would meditate every morning or exercise more, I would feel so much better." While that is true, it's also true that I would only be doing these things to avoid the depression.

So, let's just get to it. Let's go right into the heart of this depression, into the deep dark something or nothing that looms there—the core of my melancholy.

I could just blow it off as a thyroid condition, "It's just a symptom of hypothyroidism." This is just a chemical imbalance in my endocrine system that needs a doctor's attention. Does anyone have a magic pill?

I could chalk it up to losing an acquaintance today. She passed away suddenly from a brain tumor. She was my age.

Alternatively, I could drop into my center and ask, "What would you like to share that is showing up as depression and anxiety?" The hard part is sitting still long enough and without agenda to listen actually to the answer. Ok, here goes . . .

It comes from a fear that I'm going to drop the ball and fail at something important. I often juggle balls beyond my known capacity and hope not to drop them, but sometimes I do drop them, like friendships. I make "to do" lists in hopes I don't forget something important, but am overwhelmed and often don't check it.

It includes the fear that I'm going to get in trouble even though I am well-meaning. As a child, I would get in trouble for things I didn't even do! I'm always waiting for the shoe to drop. I fear IRS tax audits. I fear a recession that could cause us to lose our home and business. I fear one of my staff will quit and I won't have enough help. I fear that my health or my spouse's health will fail and we won't know what to do.

I fear that as I come "out" as a mystical mermaid, people will try to harm me. Historically, burning at the stake or being stoned was the fate of women, who come out as powerful, beautiful and spoke the truth. I feel this history in my bones. I fear that people will try to judge me by saying that this is all "new age mumbo jumbo," and "weird." This happened a lot in my childhood because of my fundamentalist church. It was painful not to be fully self-expressed and be perceived as wrong.

I fear rejection from others similar to what I felt as a child on the playground when I wasn't "cool enough" to play with them. I gave up trying to be cool and decided I'd rather be kind to others, but it didn't stop the hurt.

(Two weeks later, I reread this journal and felt these thoughts were not trapping me any longer—just by bringing them to the forefront, they had lost their power, and I laugh at them when they arise now.)

# EXHIBIT

## 7 Helpful tips on getting out of bed earlier

1. **GO TO BED EARLIER** so you get plenty of sleep. Most of us need less sleep than we think, but many of us feel tired because of overeating at night. We spend the night digesting a heavy meal rather than rejuvenating.

2. **LET DINNER BE YOUR LIGHTEST MEAL AND STOP EATING AFTER 8 PM.** New habits are easier if supported by those around you. If you have a current pattern of staying up late watching TV with someone, you will need to ask them to turn off the TV and help you get to bed on time until your new habit is established.

3. Now is the time to learn to **MAKE SOME "UNREASONABLE REQUESTS".** Requests for support are not actually unreasonable, but any request of others can feel unreasonable if like me, you've spent most of your life putting the needs of others first. Now, it's time to put you first until you heal and get used to self-care. Enroll others in your plan, so they know what you're up to and can support you in making it happen.

4. Ideally, wake up naturally, but until that begins to happen, **SET A FRIENDLY ALARM** and place it half way across the room. Friendly means that it does not "alarm" you. DESCRIBE

HOW TO SET SMART PHONE ALARM SOUND. Gentle waking is important for your health because we do not want your cortisol levels to spike at any time during the day unless you are being chased by a tiger. Cortisol spikes are like a rush of adrenaline, like spending on a credit card, and leave me reaching for a sugar boost to cope with life when I drop later.

5. **WAKE UP KINDLY.** If feeling groggy, give yourself what it needs at that moment. In my case, I like to take three deep diaphragmatic breaths to oxygenate my blood followed by stretching and twisting my body under the covers (much like a cat does). These activities actually feel good and get my blood circulating while I'm still warm. (You could even do your daily affirmations, readings and journaling under the covers before getting out of bed if that works best for you). Then I like to take a shower or at least place a hot wet wash cloth on my face to "steam my eyeballs open" as my grandmother used to say. I have to brush my teeth. Then I normally have a big glass of water and make myself a warm cup of healthy tea. I wrap up in my comfy robe and pajamas and find a comfortable quiet place where I can dive into the 13 Steps uninterrupted.

6. **PHYSICAL SUPPORT.**

   a. Moving our bodies (sometimes called exercise) usually increases metabolism and gets energy flowing. Get moving.

   b. Some of us suffer from sleep apnea and don't know it. We can't understand why we're tired all the time. If you're falling asleep all the time, you may not be getting enough oxygen at night. Be sure to get tested and treated for this! It can save your life.

7. **HAVE AN INSPIRING REASON TO WAKE UP.** If you don't feel inspired to jump out of bed and start your day, make up a good reason. Find one thing you're looking forward to that day or create one! It's usually our passions that make us swing our feet joyfully out of bed in the mornings. Sometimes I have to make something up—like that the universe is waiting to surprise and delight me, and I have to get up to open my many presents and notice the every day miracles. The universe thinks every day is like Christmas, and I can surprise and delight others too. Make up a new game that inspires you, like how many people you can make laugh in one day. Get creative. I like to show up at the beach in my mermaid tail and say that I'm a real mermaid, and this is not a costume. I can grant wishes that way.

# Endnotes

[i] While the origins of this oft-repeated story are somewhat unclear, a search for "There Must Be a Pony Somewhere," at *www.quoteinvestigator* shows that the story may come from a 1949 speech delivered by a President of Union College who addressed Rotary International.

[ii] Jelaluddin Rumi, Coleman Barks, *The Essential Rumi* (San Francisco, California, Harper, 1995) p.36

[iii] Joe Vitale and Ihaleakala Hew Len, *Zero Limits: The Secret System For Wealth, Health, Peace and More* ( Hoboken, NJ: John Wiley and Sons, 2007)

[iv] Michèle Hozer, Sugar Coated—*How The Food Industry Seduced The World One Spoonful At A Time,* directed by Michèle Hozer, video (2015, Telefilm Canada, distributed by Films Transit International and White Pine Pictures) online video.

[v] Allan Heinberg and Zack Snyder, *Wonder Woman*, IMDb, Patty Jenkins, director, (2017, Burbank, California, Warner Brothers) Film.

[vi] Hank Wesselman, *The Bowl of Light; Ancestral Wisdom From A Hawaiian Shaman* (Boulder, Colorado, Sounds True Inc., 2011)

[vii] Masaru Emoto, *Messages From Water, Vol. 1,* (Japan, Hadu Kyoiku Sha Co., Ltd., 1999)

[viii] R. Arvigo and N. Epstein, Spiritual Bathing: *Healing Rituals and Traditions from Around the World* (Berkley, California, Celestial Arts, 2003).

[ix] Carolyn Coker Ross, "Why Do Women Hate Their Bodies?," *World of Psychology,* https://psychcentral.com/blog/archives/2012/06/02/why-do-women-hate-their-bodies/

[x] Malala Yousafzai and Christina Lamb, *I am Malala; The Girl Who Stood Up For Education And Was Shot By the Taliban* (New York, New York, Weidenfeld & Nicolson, 2013)

xi Louise Hay, *You Can Heal Your Life* (Carlsbad, California, Hay House, 1984).

xii Jimmy Cliff, "I Can See Clearly Now the Rain is Gone," by Johnny Nash, 1993 Epic Record Labels, single compact disk

xiii Paul Reps, *Zen Flesh Zen Bones,* (North Clarendon, VT, Tuttle Publishing) 1985

xiv Deborah L. Price, *Money Magic: Unleashing Your True Potential for Prosperity and Fulfillment* (Novato, California, New World Library)

xv Kahlil Gibran, *The Prophet,* (New York, New York, Alfred Knoff, Inc.) Eighty-Third Printing, p. 36

xvi Suzanne Collins, *The Hunger Games,* IDMb, Robin Bissell and Suzanne Collins, directors (2012, Lionsgate Films) film

xvii The Drowning Man story is in various forms on the internet and in books, but there is no known original source for the story.

xviii This is an oral story handed down to me with no known source for the original.

xix Gloria G. Guzman, "Household Income 2016," *United States Census Bureau,* https://www.census.gov/content/dam/Census/library/publications/2017/acs/acsbr16-02.pdf

xx Erin El Issa, "American Household Credit Card Debt Study," *Nerd Wallet Inc.,* 2017, https://www.nerdwallet.com/blog/credit-card-data/average-credit-card-debt-household/

xxi Maureen St. Germain, *Waking up in 5D: A Practical Guide to Multidimensional Transformation* (Rochester, Vermont, Bear & Company, 2017)

xxii Albert Brooks and Monica Johnson, *The Muse,* IDMb, Albert Brooks, director (1999, October Films) Film.

xxiii Glennon Doyle Melton, *Carry On, Warrior: The Power of Embracing Your Messy, Beautiful Life* (NY, NY, Scribner, 2013) xxiv Tosha Silver and Christianne Northrup, *Outrageous Openness: Letting The Divine Take The Lead* (New York, New York, Atria Paperback, 2014)

xxv Mohandas Gandhi and Homer A. Jack, *The Wit and Wisdom of Gandhi—Eastern Philosophy and Religion* (Mineola, New York, Dover, 2005)

xxvi Tejvan Pettinger, "Is That So?—Zen Story," *Happiness Will Follow You—Self Improvement for Daily Life,* August 2008, http://www.srichinmoybio.co.uk/blog/life/is-that-so-zen-story/

xxvii Laurel Thatcher Ulrich, *Well-behaved Women Seldom Make History* (New York, New York, Vintage Books) 2007

xxviii Josh Grobin, You Raise Me Up, Lyrics by Brendan Graham and Rolf Loveland, 2003 on Chaser, Reprise Records, 2004, compact disc.

xxxvii Jeff Brumbeau and Gail DeMarcken, *The Quilt Maker's Gift* (Broadway, New York, Scholastic Press,2000)

xxxviii Alan Christianson, *The Adrenal Reset Diet* (New York, New York, Harmony Books, 2014)

xxxix "Taiji's Drive Season Over," *Rick O'Berry's Dolphin Project,* February 28, 2017, https://dolphinproject.com/blog/breaking-taijis-drive-season-over/

xl Forks Over Knives, LLC, https://www.forksoverknives.com/app/#gs.yFLcBUo

xli Rosanna Ferrera (http://naturalwaysinstitute.com/) and Linda Goolsby (fresh_start_today@yahoo.com)

xlii Gary Chapman, The 5 Love Languages (Chicago, Illinois, Northfield Publishing,1992)

xliii *Satyagraha,* Encyclopedia Britannica (2015), www.britannica.com/topic/satyagraha-philosophy

xliv Ricado Semler, "How to Run a Company With Almost No Rules" (presentation, Ted Talks Global 2014) https://www.ted.com/talks/

ricardo_semler_how_to_run_a_company_with_almost_no_rules

[xlv] Steven Pinker, *How the Mind Works* (New York, New York, Norton & Company, 2009)

[xlvi] Forks Over Knives, MP4 (2014), online video www.forksoverknives.com/the-film/#gs.fPIeEgs

[xlvii] Joe Cross, *"Fat, Sick and Nearly Dead"* (Reboot With Joe—Juicing for Weight-loss with Joe Cross) www.rebootwithjoe.com/watch-fat-sick-and-nearly-dead

[xlviii] http://DivingIntoTheDivineFeminine.com

[xlix] Ariel Spilsbury, *The 13 Moon Oracle A Journey of Archetypal Faces of the Divine Feminine* (Mandela Publishing, 2006) p. 172.